Going the Extra

Just an ordinary sort of chap – that's how Bob Hain would describe himself. All those whose lives he's touched probably wouldn't agree. Ever since he was a young man, growing up in Dorset, he's been unable to refuse a new challenge or a request for help. This desire to 'go the extra mile' has taken him, among other places, into the boxing ring, onto the stage and the dance floor, into the classroom and the church, and finally to Africa.

After marrying his childhood sweetheart, Nel Morgan, Bob, employed by the National Provincial Bank (later NatWest), was sent to work in various branches in the South of England before settling in rural Oxfordshire. When the bank offered him the opportunity to work instead for the Leonard Cheshire Foundation he accepted without hesitation.

After a fund-raising position, he transferred to the Cheshire Homes Aids to the Disabled section (CHAD), overseeing the supply of essential medical equipment to Homes overseas. He made it a 'hands-on' job, and soon it was no surprise to the villagers of Stonesfield to see Bob and Nel turning their cars into their drive before unloading the latest stash of wheelchairs, in various states of disrepair, into the garden. After being mended, the chairs were soon winging their way to places as far away as Indonesia and Swaziland.

In 1999 Bob was invited to Buckingham Palace to receive an MBE for 'Services to Disabled People Overseas'.

Going the Extra Mile
The story of Bob Hain, MBE

As told by Rosemary Cleaver

Bob Hain

APPLE TREE BOOKS

This book may be ordered from bookshops or from
Apple Tree Books, Churchfields, Stonesfield, Witney,
Oxfordshire OX29 8PP
01993 891204

e-mail: appletree@cleaver.eclipse.co.uk
credit card orders should be phoned to 01993 891204

First published in 2014 by
Apple Tree Books
Churchfields, Stonesfield, Witney
Oxfordshire OX29 8PP

ISBN 978 0 9568589 1 7

The right of Rosemary Cleaver to be identified as author of this work has been asserted in accordance with the Copyright, Designs and Patents Act 1988.

All rights reserved. No part of this publication may be produced, stored in a retrieval system or transmitted in any form or by any means electronic, mechanical, photocopying or otherwise without the prior permission in writing of the publisher.

Cover photograph by Charles Green

Printed in England by
Berforts Information Press Ltd.

CONTENTS

    Prologue
1. A country child in Dorset
2. School, church and a prophecy
3. Wartime hop-picking and learning to box
4. Starting work in the bank and signing on for the Army
5. Training at Inverness before Officer Selection trials
6. An eventful Dorset dance follows a Gibraltar posting
7. Teaching in Berlin and back to banking after demob
8. Bob and Nel marry and enjoy their new life
9. A few moves before settling in Oxfordshire
10. Bob leads a Youth Club and Nel forms a Choral Society
11. Acting and dancing, a playing field and a new village hall
12. Two festivals and a Tennis Club
13. The children leave home
14. Leaving the bank for new challenges
15. Good fortune for CHAD and an important visitor
16. A visit to Zimbabwe and a Royal Investiture
17. On safari – Africa again
18. The Millennium project and another new home

Prologue

Bob Hain, dressed in a brand new suit, tried to make sense of it all. He was one of a large group of people standing in an annexe just to the left of the Buckingham Palace Ballroom. If he peered through the arched doorway in front of him he could see the rich crimson carpet covering the floor and the dais where, quite soon now, a member of the Royal Family, or even the Queen of England would stand.

Was this really happening? Had he really come here to be made a Member of the Most Excellent order of the British Empire? Thinking that it sounded faintly ridiculous, Bob smiled. He felt he was an everyday kind of person, whereas some of these people were well-known and seemed far more important. Why, only just now he'd been chatting with an England fast bowler while they were waiting. Looking towards the grand, white and gold ballroom, a glimpse of a red, black and gold uniform told Bob that the five members of the Yeoman of the Guard had taken their places on the platform.

Smartly-dressed people were sitting on plush red chairs. Three of these would be members of his own family – his wife Nel, their son Rob and daughter-in-law Maggie. Dear Nel, he'd known her since they were small children. He pictured her young, smiling face as they danced the 'Rufty-Tufty' in the Dorset sunshine. They'd come such a long way together. And what on earth would his friends have said about this – those boys who'd paddled around and fished with him in the River Stour? Or his army mates? They'd probably pull his leg a bit – hobnobbing with royalty! He wondered if the people in the bank had heard and hoped some of his old customers would be pleased.

It was thanks to the bank that he was here today. Bob always relished a challenge; he found it difficult to refuse even when he wasn't quite suited to it – like the time he'd ended up getting really beaten in the boxing ring. So when the NatWest Bank offered him the chance to move over to charity work he accepted it straight away. And he had loved working for the Leonard Cheshire Foundation, be it raising funds or sending hundreds of wheelchairs to Cheshire Homes overseas. He knew it was appreciated because he'd had plenty of letters to say so, and he'd been thanked by some wonderful people. But it had been a pleasure, and now, just for doing something he'd really enjoyed, he was going to be given a medal.

The musicians, who'd been playing quietly at the back of the ballroom, fell silent. Bob saw a small, elegant, grey-haired lady enter the room wearing a blue dress and two rows of pearls. Two proud Ghurka officers protected her on either side. Everyone rose as the band played the National Anthem. It was time.

'And whosoever shall compel thee to go a mile, go with him twain.'

St Matthew chapter 5, verse 41

Bob in 1930, four years old

CHAPTER 1

On 22 October 1926, in the lovely village of Durweston, Dorset, a little boy was born. His delighted parents, Reg and Mary Hain, called him Victor Arthur, a brother for their small daughter Ena, aged just 21 months.

Reg himself had been born into a large family where his father's wages had to feed and clothe seven children. Like many young men in Durweston he went off, full of determination, to fight in the Great War. He survived the harrowing experience but was brought home wounded and hospitalised in Southampton.

Here he was visited by a young woman, Mary Florence Stroud. She was one of a group of people who, out of kindness, felt it their duty to go to the hospital and talk with these men who had been through so much trauma for their country. They would take little treats to the patients and try to bring some light and laughter into the hospital wards. Reg began to look forward to visits from the pretty young woman who introduced herself as Mary. She told him she worked in the rag trade and was a buyer for the firm of Tyrell and Green in Southampton. Lying on his hard, hospital bed, Reg spent a lot of time thinking about Mary. Born in the great city of London, she had grown up far removed from the simple country ways of Reg and his family. She had a good job and seemed so full of life and enthusiasm – was there any hope for him? It appeared there was.

When Reg left the hospital and was fit for work he became a jobbing builder. He and Mary started courting and after what he thought was a suitable time lapse, he asked her to marry him. Getting Mary to agree to this was not quite so easy, but Reg was a determined chap and eventually Mary said yes. They married in 1923 and went to live in Reg's home village of Durweston, three miles from Blandford Forum. The village was owned by Lord Portman who lived with his immediate family just outside in The Mansion (now Bryanston School). Portmans also lived in Knighton House and Portman Lodge in Durweston.

In January 1925 the couple had their first baby, Ena, who was destined to spend her adult life in the USA. The next year, in October, her brother Victor was born. For five years the two children played happily together, but the family hadn't finished growing. In 1931 Ena and Victor were excited by the arrival of a little sister, Betty, to help care for. Then, when Betty had begun toddling around and Ena and Victor were feeling quite grownup, along came Kathleen in 1933. Now there were four playmates and the family was complete.

Durweston School: Miss Garlic's class in 1936. Bob and Nel are at the back, Bob third from the right and Nel far right

Victor rather liked his special position as the only boy in the family. His little sisters started to call him 'Bubby'. The name stuck and as the children grew up it became 'Bob' and Bob was called Victor no more.

When a village did not have a school, children would frequently have to travel to get an education, but Bob and his sisters were fortunate in that Durweston had its own primary school, just a short walk away from their home. There were two classes, one for infants and one for the older children. Bob enjoyed school and had lots of friends. One of his friends was a girl called Nel Morgan, who came in every day from nearby Bryanston. In those days Bob had no idea that she would turn out to be someone very special in his life.

When the children reached the upper class they loved their teacher, Miss Garlic. In fact Nel, who sat next to Bob, often thought that he was a bit of a teacher's pet. The class performed many school plays and pantomimes and he always seemed to be chosen for the star parts: while Bob swished his cloak as Prince Charming, Nel just fluttered around the edges as a fairy or a flower. But she could see that he had a talent for acting so didn't mind too much.

Bob and Nel were partners in the country dancing class. They loved scampering round the room as they danced the 'Rufty-Tufty', 'Sellinger's Round' or 'Gathering Peascods'. When they were ten years old all the children were taken to Bovington Camp to enjoy the huge space and dance with many others from schools all over the county. It was a great success. The Durweston dancers felt exhilarated as they leapt and skipped across the wide sweep of soft, green grass in the breezy sunshine.

The infants were taught by Miss Beak and Miss Beak had in her home a wireless set. In January 1936, when Bob was nine years old, King George V died. The funeral was broadcast to the nation and Miss Garlic's class trooped from what they called 'The Big Room', past the wondering infants and along the village street to Miss Beak's house. Here, sitting on the floor and subdued by being in a teacher's home, Bob and his classmates stared around the room with wide eyes while Miss Beak switched on the wireless. The broadcast began and they listened to the long, melancholy service with serious expressions on their young faces. Nearly all of them attended church and Sunday School so the hymns and prayers were not too unfamiliar, but no doubt some still found it quite difficult to understand what they were hearing.

Durweston School in 2014

The school observed the usual festivals of Christmas, Easter, Harvest and in those days Empire Day, but a big favourite was Shrove Tuesday –

Pancake Day. Each year the whole school, along with their teachers, walked round the village, calling at the big houses and singing this rhyme:

> Here we come a-shroving
> For a piece of pancake,
> Or a bit of knuckle cheese
> Of your own making.
> Blow the fire, hit the pan
> For we be come a-shroving.

Then the owner of the house would give the children some money, the most coming from the Portman residences. One village house was known to the pupils as 'Ha'penny House' because the owner always gave them a halfpenny. (Durweston school still keeps up the tradition of 'shroving', but now the children take bunches of flowers round to villagers and are given little treats to eat in return.)

Indeed, the Portman family was most generous to the village. Every year Lady Portman gave each pupil one shilling (now only 5p but a huge amount to a child in the 1930s) to be spent on a day out in Weymouth. Lord Portman arranged this for the villagers, with children travelling free of charge and the adults paying just a nominal sum. Most families did not go on holiday so the annual village trip to the seaside was an event awaited with huge excitement and anticipation. People from the surrounding villages were invited too so when the great day arrived, five charabancs from Sprackling's transport firm stood waiting to take the chattering, laughing crowd on their journey. As they drove along in the open-topped vehicle from Dorchester and crested the hill, a great shout went up from the children, "I can see the sea!" The excitement grew even more and in a short while they arrived on the promenade.

Everyone spilled out of the charabancs. The grownups glanced up at the clock, erected near the sea in 1887 to mark the occasion of Queen Victoria's Golden Jubilee, and used by thousands of day-trippers ever since to keep a check on the time before gathering up their buckets, spades and sunhats and running for the bus home. Down on the sand the children couldn't decide what to do first. Should they make a sandcastle? Rush into the sea? Spend some of their money on a donkey ride? Look for the Punch and Judy show? Invariably they chose to pull off their shoes and stockings and run across the smooth sand into the sea. Shrieks of "Oh, it's cold!" filled the air for the first few seconds but they soon became accustomed to the temperature, which, on the edge of the sea in Weymouth Bay with its gently lapping summer waves, was very pleasant.

Many of the adults hired deckchairs and carried them to a spot on the

Weymouth, always a great place for a family day out

sand from where they could keep an eye on their children. Bob and his friends, dry again after their dip in the sea, carefully tipped up their buckets to make castles and buried their feet and sometimes each other in the sand. Then there would be games of cricket, donkey rides and sandwiches with more than a touch of grit in them before they went to shout at Mr Punch, Judy, the policeman and the crocodile.

All too soon, the wonderful day was drawing to a close. There was a last-minute rush to buy a small souvenir or, for those who had spent their shilling, to find a shell or a bit of seaweed, and then it was back to the charabancs for the journey home. Tired children would chatter gaily at first and even sing a few songs, but then a satisfied stillness would descend on the passengers and the toddlers and younger children would fall asleep.

Back in the village, everyone clambered off their charabanc, suddenly wide awake again and calling goodnight to whomever they could see. Tonight they would sleep the deep, but not quite dreamless, sleep that follows a day full of fresh air and fun.

CHAPTER 2

Usually, teachers did not have high academic expectations from country children, knowing that very few would pass their Scholarship examination. But Miss Dosell, who taught the infants, had always had great hopes for Bob. She took him aside one day and said, "You know, you're doing very well at school. If you work just a little bit harder you'll be able to pass the exam and go to grammar school."

Bob thought on this and decided that yes, he would really try hard during the months leading up to the examination. It worked. He passed. September 1937 saw the new pupil cycling the three miles from Durweston to Blandford Grammar School. Like Bob, most children from the surrounding villages arrived at school on their bikes, although those from Sturminster Newton travelled by train on the Somerset and Dorset Railway. Grammar school was very different from the small village school Bob had left behind but he soon settled in, enjoyed his lessons and began to make friends.

During the long summer holidays he still played in the fields

Nel's parents, Harry and Nell Morgan, outside their Bryanston shop

surrounding Durweston, and paddled and swam in the River Stour which ran past the village. Digging at the edges of the river soon revealed the excellent sticky clay which was so useful for building dams and all those other structures that would hopefully make the water deeper or trap fish. Minnows and sticklebacks could be scooped out with a net on a stick, put into a jam jar and taken home where they would probably lead a puzzlingly short life. Bob, like all his friends, spent much of his childhood out of doors with legs and arms brown from the sun and the mud, but unlike most of the other boys, he was now at grammar school and had to fit in something called 'homework' to his busy days.

Nel had not passed her Scholarship Exam but was really keen to go to Blandford as her friend had done. Eventually, two years later, she was able to join him. At that time it was possible to pay to go to grammar schools and Nel's parents decided that the village shop they owned was doing well enough to pay for their daughter's education. So Nel and Bob picked up their easy friendship where they had left it and spread it to include the young people who would spend the next few years working and playing alongside them.

Some teachers are remembered for their enthusiasm; others for their kindness and understanding; still more for the fear they instilled in us. But we can always recall the ones who were a source of amusement. Tom Hughes was one of those. Mr Hughes taught biology and was famous for his window-gazing. Teaching the class, he would stop speaking part-way through a sentence, saying something like, "That's particularly true in the case of ... in the case of ..." The children waited expectantly, but Tom would be quite still and gazing through the window. No-one could see anything of particular interest outside that might have caught Mr Hughes' attention. Stifled giggling always spread through the class, especially when this interlude became a regular occurrence. Eventually the teacher's attention returned to them but it was always difficult to continue listening now with their previous concentration.

The headteacher at Blandford Grammar was a Mr Jimmy Stott, but while Bob was at school Mr Stott, although only in his mid-forties, died suddenly. The headship was taken over by Tom Hughes, as a senior teacher. It was not the best appointment. Administration was not something that Mr Hughes found easy and it took up a great deal of his time. The biology classes saw less and less of their teacher, his powers of concentration diminished even more, and Bob, like quite a number of his friends, was to fail the biology exam when it came to School Certificate time.

Both Bob and Nel agreed that Mr Watkins, Sam, was a wonderful teacher. He taught English and was a big influence on them both. He was kind and had an infectious enthusiasm for his subject and his pupils looked forward to his classes – a teacher who would always be the subject of positive reminiscence.

Bob enjoyed school. He liked most of the subjects and worked hard. He was not a particularly natural sportsman but he played soccer and cricket and did his very best for the teams and Mr Chappell, the teacher. So schooldays were busy but there was still time for other things back in Durweston.

From an early age Bob had attended church, beginning with Sunday School. When he grew a little he joined the church choir along with a number of the boys from his school. They had a good choirmaster in Mr Winsor whose pay came from that very generous person, Lady Portman. When that lady entered the church on a Sunday morning, the congregation knew they must not sit in either the row in front of her or the one behind, in case she should catch a cold or similar from the villagers. Lady Portman did not attend St Nicholas every week but divided her time between Durweston and its sister church, St Martin's in Bryanston.

Later, when Bob was in his teens, the rector, Bertie Rosson, asked him if he would like to be an occasional altar server. This position was already taken on Sundays, but there were services during the week and even on Saturdays from time to time, so during school holidays Bob was happy to

St Nicholas Church, Durweston

help out. And after the service there was breakfast at the vicarage across the road. It was a big, rather grand house and it was always quite exciting to be eating there instead of at home. The house sat on a rise, a driveway climbing up to a large landscaped garden which could be enjoyed by all the villagers when Bertie opened it up for school fetes and anything else that needed a good open space.

The rector ministered to the two villages. Bertie always had time to chat and spent much of his time visiting his parishioners. A kind man with a great sense of humour, small in stature but big in personality, he was a very popular caller and loved by all the villagers – whether they attended church or not. Bob got along very well with him and Mrs Hain could see that the Revd Rosson was a good influence on her son, although she hardly ever went to church herself. So he was always welcome in the Hain household as he was in most others.

One day Nel came home from school to find Bertie perched on a chair in the shop. He and her mother had been discussing the friendship between her daughter and young Bob Hain. "You'll find, Mrs Morgan – that that'll be a case!" said the rector.

"Oh Mr Rosson!" exclaimed Nel's mother, "She's only ten years old!" Bertie gave her a smile that said 'Well, just you wait and see', and with Nel's entrance the subject crept away and talk turned to questions about the business of a school day.

CHAPTER 3

When Bob was nearly thirteen, war was declared. Although nothing had happened to affect life in Durweston there was a general feeling of excitement amongst the boys and young men. The overwhelming thought was that Britain would of course win; the option of losing was not considered. In fact very soon posters began to appear to that effect, telling people not to even think of defeat. Older men who had been through the First World War were quieter. Their thoughts could not turn easily from the horrors so many had experienced.

The following year, 1940, saw the constant bombardment of the country by German planes during the Battle of Britain. In September Bob and his school friends Ian Dunne, a Scottish lad who was later to die in the war, and Gordon Kaile who was good at soccer and became one of the Notts Forest players, joined with a few others to cycle to Bentley in Hampshire for the annual hop harvest.

Always happy to try anything new, the boys had heard in school that there was a shortage of people to pick the hops and thought they would earn a nice bit of pocket money by offering their services. Two or three miles out of Blandford Bob's tyre had a puncture. The only thing to do was to push the bike back to the town where Reggie Acourt had a cycle shop. This took quite a while and the repair cost Bob the princely sum of half a crown (or two shillings and sixpence: 25p) but the group had waited for him and they all set off again to Bentley.

On arrival at the hop fields the boys were shown their accommodation which was in large bell tents, each holding six people. After depositing their belongings they started picking straight away and found that their fellow-pickers were highly experienced gypsies. Watching these people working, the boys were amazed at the speed with which they stripped the hop cones from the bines. Bob and Ian tried their very best but had to pick each cone individually and by the end of the day were disappointed by the small amounts in their baskets. It had been hard work and they slept well in their tent after a good plain meal from the farm canteen.

Every day the boys tried to improve their skills. In the skies overhead a huge battle was being fought and many aircraft flew over the pickers as they worked. Fortunately, people in hop fields were of no interest to German planes and the schoolboys couldn't afford to waste too much time gazing upwards.

They all picked as fast as they could for almost a week. But at the end of their employment the farmer looked at the boys, standing in a hopeful line to receive their pay, and said, "I'm sorry but you've only earned just enough to pay for your keep – nothing extra." With that he turned to the gypsies and counted out their money. Bob wrapped his sore fingers round the handlebars and, as he rode off with the group, knew he had no plans to return to Hampshire the following year.

The Durweston Boy Scout Group was called 'The Pigeons'. As soon as he was old enough Bob had joined the group which met in the old brewery. The building had been unoccupied for some years previously and the Scout Association now decided that it needed attention in the form of a new floor.

A local carpenter, Billy Adlem, was consulted. Billy said that if the boys would help he would show them how to lay a new wooden floor. This was an exciting project for them and the group worked well together. Before long their big meeting room looked like new. However, the scouts were unable to enjoy their smart quarters for long because a week or two later an army battalion marched into the village and promptly occupied the whole of the old brewery. After that, the boys met when and where they could, knowing that the soldiers had an important job to do and feeling that the group had helped a little towards the War Effort.

Bob could be described as a keen scout and enjoyed lighting fires, camping and all the preparations that went with it. When his leader, Captain Browne, told the boys there was to be a new activity coming up, the young man was keen to hear all about it. The pursuit was boxing and a team would be needed to take part in tournaments. Bob, always willing to have a go, volunteered for the team and began to 'train'. The first contest the boys entered took place in Poole. Tall and slim and describing himself as 'ponderously slow', Bob was paired against a chunky, fair-haired lad who was much faster in the ring. This boy won the contest easily, on points.

Undeterred by his first setback, Bob volunteered his services against a scout team from Somerset. Once again, he was much slower than his opponent and sustained heavy punishment during the first two rounds. Coming out for the final round Bob was determined to make amends and went 'bald-headed' for a knock-out. It didn't work. The Durweston contestant left himself wide open to a fierce battering. But although he could feel the flesh on his face beginning to swell alarmingly it appeared that all was not as bad as he feared: Bob won a medal for being the best loser of the evening. His pleasure, however, was short-lived. After the contest, the organisers supplied the boys with a wonderfully aromatic supper of sausage and mash. Because of his painful, swollen jaws the wounded fighter could hardly eat anything.

In June 1942 Bob went to Bournemouth with Bertie Rosson. Bertie was easy to talk to, being keen on football like Bob and a Luton Town supporter. The rector needed to visit the town to buy some books and invited the young man along for company. After they had completed the business, Bob enjoyed a good lunch with Bertie at a restaurant in Westover Road. It was a sunny summer's day and, feeling pleasantly full, the two strolled across to the cliff top and stood looking out to sea. As their eyes scanned the horizon they spotted three distant aeroplanes heading inland.

Bob said to Bertie, "Look – it's our lads coming back from a sweep!" They shaded their eyes with their hands and watched as the planes edged nearer to the cliff. As they reached the coast the three planes climbed upwards, revealing crosses in the fuselage and swastikas on the wings. The pilots swooped overhead, each one dropping one bomb which had been slung under the fuselage. Bertie and Bob gasped in horror as the bombs exploded, two falling harmlessly but the third striking the Anglo-Swiss Hotel. The aeroplanes, Messerschmidt 109s, turned immediately and raced back across the channel. It was all over very quickly but left many casualties in its wake.

Bob, along with many others, also witnessed the destruction of a Dornier bomber over the Milldown near Blandford. Nicknamed 'The Flying Pencil', these planes were notoriously difficult to shoot down because of their long, slender shape. On this particular day Bob was at home when he heard the sound of aeroplanes. As always he hurried out into the garden to see what was happening. Overhead, the Dornier Do 17 was being stalked by a pair of British Hawker Hurricanes. There was no escape for the Pencil. After a minute or so, shots fired from both above and below hit their target and the German plane swooped down towards the fields. Somehow the pilot managed to level the aircraft and it landed bumpily.

The crew, injured but alive, were taken to Blandford Cottage Hospital. This was not the ideal outcome for one villager, well-known for shouting, rather than speaking, his mind who bawled, "We got wives and children here – shoot the b...s!" Some people were very keen to collect war momentoes and Bob and his friends would hunt around for bits of schrapnel after the enemy had offloaded their unused bombs in the open countryside. But the local people were quite disturbed to discover that while the airmen from the Dornier were in the hospital a souvenir-hunter had crept in and cut off the buttons from one of their greatcoats.

These two events were to be Bob's only taste of the war up close, even though he was to join the Home Guard and then the army.

During that summer of 1942, Canon Bertie Rosson called on Bob's mum Mary to discuss something very important. He knew that the young man had just completed his School Certificate exams and had noticed that there was a vacancy for a junior clerk at the National Provincial Bank in Blandford. Not wanting Bob to miss an opportunity, Bertie had already spoken to the manager, Archie Mills, and knew he would be happy to see him. When Mary heard about it she was keen for Bob to try for the job, and although the exam results would not be known for a few weeks, an interview was arranged.

Mr Mills seemed to be impressed with Bob and employed him firstly on a temporary basis, although before long, with a School Certificate under his belt (four credits, two passes and two failures – one, of course, being biology), he was made permanent.

CHAPTER 4

Before starting his new job Bob had time for a short holiday. He chose to go and stay with Mary's friend, known as Auntie Maude, who lived in Romford, Essex and thoroughly enjoyed himself. For a few days, he was still a carefree boy, dependent on others' care and generosity, but at the same time there was an awareness and a quiet excitement inside him that a new and very different phase of his life was about to begin. Bob loved being somewhere different and savouring Auntie Maude's tasty meals, but the best thing about his visit was having to spend most nights in the air-raid shelter. With an air-raid nearly every night, this was very different from sleepy little Durweston!

But the little holiday was soon over and in August 1942 Bob Hain climbed on his bicycle and began his career in the bank. His pleasure in starting to earn his own living was great. In those days, bank workers were not well paid. In fact the honour of just being employed by a bank was thought to be almost enough in itself – the pay being a bonus. Bob's wages were 25/- (25 shillings: £1.25) a week plus 6/- (30p) extra in something called 'grant-in-aid'. This was the bank's way of increasing wages by giving a casual payment that could, in theory, be removed at any time.

Bob gave his mother 10/- (50p) a week and spent almost that amount again on weekday lunches. He could eat at the newly opened British Restaurant or Hicks', but most lunches were taken at Viner's, close to the bank, where his favourite, costing nine old pence, was beans on toast. He liked the puddings here too and sometimes treated himself to a steamed sponge or apple pie and custard. As he strolled along to the restaurant, the young man was unaware of a young woman watching him from the windows of the telephone exchange on the opposite side of the road. It was Nel Morgan who worked there as a telephonist. Bob and Nel had lost contact with each other since they left school and it was to be a year or two before their relationship was rekindled in a new way.

It was quite natural for a boy, just out of school, to start on the bottom rung of the work ladder. But although most of his tasks were quite menial to begin with, Bob knew that he was making an important contribution to the smooth running of the bank.

At each service point on the counter was a square of blotting paper secured on its firm base at each corner. When a form or cheque needed to be signed, the customer would pick up the pen nearby and dip its nib into the inkwell which was sunk into the counter. Then the paper could be turned over onto the blotter which soaked up the spare ink. On his first day Bob was told that he must renew the blotting paper every day, change the little gold-coloured pen nibs as they wore out and make sure that the inkwells were always full. This latter reminded him of school but the task felt much more important here, where customers must be looked after at all times and the efficient operation of the bank was paramount.

The bank had a staff of six, including two ladies. Archie Mills was the manager, assisted by the under manager, Mr Winter. Mr Mills rarely used his office and these two sat at the front of the large room, just behind the counter. Behind them, the more important staff worked at their desks. Most of the workers were very kind and helpful to the new employee who sat at the back of the room. Behind Bob, in a passageway, sat the telephone. The communications system was a simple one, consisting of this main phone and one extension in the manager's office.

Bob had never used a telephone before and it took him a day or so to get the hang of it. His first attempt at answering a call went something like this. As he was opening a cupboard to search for a few nibs, a sudden loud ringing noise echoed in the empty passageway. Bob glanced round the room to see a couple of the staff looking at him expectantly and nodding in the direction of the telephone. The young man dropped the nibs, his pace quickened by the insistent rings, and hurried out to pick up the receiver. "National Provincial Bank," said Bob, remembering what he had been told to say. "I'd like to speak to the manager", said a rather grand voice. "Certainly, sir. I'll just see if he's available," answered Bob, feeling rather pleased with himself. With that, he replaced the receiver and went to find Mr Mills.

Fortunately, Bob was not prone to panic and soon began to feel confident in his work, whether it was answering the telephone, occasionally making tea or, in autumn and winter, stoking up the 'Tortoise' stove. This stove was at the rear of the building and it was Bob's responsibility to keep it alight. If he was busy working and forgot to feed the fire, the room would cool down and then he would be in trouble.

But he was happy in the bank and felt grateful to Bertie for opening the door for him. A few months after he joined, Mr Winter had a word with him. "You know Bob, most of us do some kind of war work in our spare time," he said. "I'm an officer in the Home Guard here in the town. It would be nice if you could join something like that."

Bob agreed that he should do something and the Durweston Home Guard welcomed the new recruit. The battalion was in the charge of a Mr Perry who was the head teacher of the National school in Blandford. Bob found the officer's leadership a bit odd and doubted that the group would be of any help at all if there were an invasion. On training nights Mr Perry lined up the men and said something like, "Now then – what I'm going to do this evening is test your powers of perception." Once, he disappeared behind a wall and lit a cigarette. Moving on to other hiding places he set fire to little piles of various materials and left them smouldering. The battalion's job was to walk around, each man sniffing perceptively so that he could pinpoint the aromas that filled the smoky air. Bob found all this quite amusing but soldiered on, armed with his wooden 'rifle', waiting for the day when he could join the proper army.

The war seemed a distant thing, the residents of Durweston, Blandford and most of Dorset untouched by its venomous fingers. Bob felt the atmosphere was almost surreal as he cycled back and forth to the bank and carried on with his daily routine. But in 1944 Blandford was to become part of the main thoroughfare for troops and equipment travelling down from Salisbury Plain to the coast in preparation for the D-day landings.

The first thing the residents noticed was the arrival of lorries carrying tons of cement and machinery. Soldiers jumped out and were soon at work, strengthening the roads and bridges with concrete to minimise the damage that the huge tracks of heavy tanks would cause. In early June people lined the pavements to watch the first of the armoured vehicles, tanks and lorries bearing weapons, supplies and soldiers as they roared through the town.

As he watched the khaki-clad men, some stern-faced and determined, some smiling and waving and still others looking faintly bewildered, Bob knew that, very soon, he too would be wearing the uniform of the British Army. On 22 April when he was exactly seventeen and a half years old he walked into the Labour Exchange and signed on to join up. He knew that once he had reached this age he did not need his parents' permission. Not only was the young man very keen to join the army, but at the same time he was aware that if he stayed where he was there was a chance that he would be sent to work down the coal mines. Bob would not have wanted that.

At first he told no-one of his decision. When Archie Mills first heard the news a few weeks later he was surprised and did not seem pleased that Bob had kept things to himself. But he understood his employee's thinking and was rather proud of the fact that Bob had chosen the army, as he himself had been an officer in the 1914-18 war.

Bob soon received his papers from the War Office. When asked which regiment he wanted to join he had written 'Parachute Regiment' on his application form but found now that he was to be an infantry man in the Dorset Regiment. His adaptable self thought that was fine and he read that on 15 June he was to report to the 30th Infantry Training Battalion in Inverness. (It was to be many years later before Bob was told that the men chosen for Inverness were those considered worthy of fast-track training as potential officer material.) He stared at the letter. He was seventeen and he had rarely strayed outside his home village of Durweston. Now he was being asked to travel to the north of Scotland! Excitement and apprehension fought inside him. This was going to be very different.

CHAPTER 5

On June 14th, Bob's father woke him with a cup of tea at 6.30 in the morning. While Bob sat up in bed and drank it, Reg gave him some worldly advice that he felt a rookie should know. A few weeks previously, the two men had had what Bob would describe as an 'altercation', but now the wounds had healed and he knew that his Dad was proud of him. Before Reg left his son to get dressed, the two hugged each other, pleased and relieved that all was well between them. When Mary had been told of her son's intentions she was, as ever, supportive. She knew that he would have to do service at some time and accepted his decision to go now with her usual good humour.

Bob finished his breakfast, said his farewells and hurried to the Stourpaine and Durweston Halt. The train carrying him on the first leg of his journey had arrived. The driver watched him racing up the steps and laughingly called out, "You wanna get up in the mornin'!" Bob thanked him for waiting, climbed on board and sank gratefully into a seat. The engine shot steam into the air and slowly moved off. Rocking gently in the carriage, Bob wondered what lay ahead. He had left everything that was familiar to journey to a place he had only seen on a map. He couldn't think that Scotland would be like Dorset – would he even understand a Scottish accent? And his time with the Home Guard had hardly prepared him for a soldier's way of life. Oh well, time would tell.

Bob's father, Reg

Soon the train arrived at Templecombe where Bob had to wait some time for his connection to London. The journey was long and slow and the train pulled into Waterloo at dusk. In the evenings, London hid under its blackout curtains and it would have been very difficult for a stranger to the city to find his way around. Bob's saviour was Mary's brother Arthur who lived in Bexley Heath and knew London well.

Uncle Arthur was at the station to meet his nephew's train. He led Bob through the darkness to a bus waiting to go to King's Cross station. Bob adored his uncle and was very grateful for his help. All through Bob's young life Arthur had climbed on his bicycle to ride through the night to see his sister and her family in Dorset. One night a man had jumped out in front of him and demanded money. Arthur showed him his empty pockets and said, "Look old man, I haven't got any money. I've got to go down to my sister's and get some work." Then, as he climbed back on his bike, he called out with the sense of humour he shared with Mary: "Better luck next time!"

Now he sat with Bob as the bus, its headlights shaded to project only the narrowest beam of light, crawled through the black, bomb-devastated streets towards King's Cross. Bob was amazed that, somehow, they eventually arrived at the right place. Here, Arthur watched and waved as his nephew slowly went out of sight, safely inside the express train to Edinburgh.

Travelling at night, Bob could see nothing of the towns or countryside as the express raced northwards. Occasionally he would just be dozing off in his seat when the sudden smack of air from a passing train would startle him. It was difficult to sleep; the sudden small pools of light and feel of buildings of a station, the hollow roar of a tunnel and the sliding and banging of doors all added to the dreamlike quality of the night's journey.

Eventually the train steamed into Waverley station in Edinburgh. Here, Bob boarded a much slower train bound for Inverness. As he gazed at the passing hills and valleys, he noticed a number of other young men who looked as if they too were seeing this country for the first time. He was right; when the train steamed into Inverness station, he alighted with many other lads who had travelled from different parts of the British Isles. His journey had taken over 24 hours.

Army transport waited outside the station. The new recruits piled onto the lorries for the last leg of their journeys. After a short ride they all took their first steps onto Scottish tarmac, where, standing as straight as they knew how, they were 'welcomed' sharply by RSM Kirby. Bedding kit was issued to them: to lie on, the usual trio of army 'biscuits' with their unrelenting filling; two sheets and a blanket. Then the young men were measured for that which would make them feel much more like soldiers – the army uniform. Whilst sorting out their gear and making up their beds they began the process of getting to know each other, introducing themselves in a wide variety of regional accents.

Bob shared a bunk bed with a lad from Yorkshire. This young fellow apparently had been in a bit of trouble and been told by the authorities, "Right then – it's the army or borstal for you. Make your choice!" A very different kind of lad from Bob, he could be belligerent at times and Bob had to stop his eyebrows from shooting up when he heard the streams of colourful language. Nevertheless, the two got to know each other well and despite their differences and his companion's insistence that Bob used the far more awkward, very low bottom bunk, Private Hain found him a good mate.

Training began. The sergeants and sergeant majors were a mixed bunch, some quite lenient but the rest much sharper. The RSM was the one to be feared, although Bob believed that his frequent threats of charges and firing squads disguised a very decent chap. After a few days, one of the Scottish sergeants decided that there was too much swearing in the barracks and told the new recruits that it just wouldn't do. Without thinking, Bob blurted out, "Well, the NCOs don't set a very good example!" There was a moment's silence as the sergeant slowly fixed his piercing blue eyes onto those of his young trainee. "Don't you dare to criticise the NCOs," was his cutting reply. Bob had learned something about the revered army hierarchy.

Half of the time was spent on the parade ground learning foot drill, or 'square bashing' as it was called by generations of soldiers. When the men were not being shouted into shape by Sergeant Major Kirby, they would be on one of their route marches across Culloden Moor. The moor was a wild and windy place and even though it was summer, it could feel quite cold and bleak. One day Bob fell into a stream when his foot slipped off a stepping stone. He was soaked from the waist down but there was no chance for his heavy trousers to dry out. The platoon marched on until it reached a large barn which had been given over to the army. Bob was glad to get inside and have a meal. But his clothes were still very wet and the wind whistled through the cracks and under the doors of the old barn.

Bob shivered with cold as he tried to settle down for the night. Sleeping was very difficult and after a few hours he realised that he felt ill. He knew he had a temperature and, when he got up to report his plight to the officer in charge, he could hardly stand. The officer looked him over. Although he thought Bob looked very groggy, he nevertheless warned the private that if he was found to be 'pulling a fast one', he'd be straight on a charge. After that, the man arranged to send him back to Inverness. As it grew light, Bob was driven to Raigmore hospital, which was then only a small cottage hospital on the outskirts of Inverness, where he was stripped of his wet clothes and given a warm bed. A doctor diagnosed influenza and the young soldier was given treatment and care for the next three days, after which he was declared fit enough to be sent back to barracks.

Soon after his return, Bob was called in to the CO's office. Puzzled as to why he had been summoned, he made his way there and knocked politely on the door. He did not have to wait long. Straight away, the CO told him that he'd been chosen for possible officer training and arrangements had been made for him to appear before a selection board in Edinburgh. Well, this was a turn-up for the books; Bob Hain from Durweston – an officer? Bob would try his very best.

He arrived in Edinburgh to find that he was one of 16 men to appear before the Board. Part of the university area had been taken over for the selection process. Firstly, the candidates had to undergo a series of initiative tests, after which each would give a 15-minute address to the board on a subject of their choice. Some of the tests were physical, others mental, and after some tests the soldiers had to give their votes to whomever they judged to be the least successful. There was a pond in the grounds with a large, semi-submerged stone in the centre. The men were roped together and each had to leap across to the stone and from there to the other side of the pond. When Bob's turn came he pulled rather too hard on the rope as he jumped, with the result that the previous man fell back into the pond. As the soldier heaved himself out, Bob watched the water streaming off his heavy khaki trousers and thought to himself, 'Well, I know where his vote's going!'

When the time came for the 15-minute talks, Bob knew he must know his subject well. He chose something with which he was very familiar: the rules of Association Football. When he stood before the Board he was nervous but thought it went reasonably well. But, when speaking afterwards to some of the other candidates who'd listened to him after completing their own addresses, he felt his confidence beginning to ebb away a little. They seemed to be far more worldly than him and had spoken about such subjects as hunting, foreign travel and rugby. How could he, a country lad who had hardly left Durweston, compete with them? Oh well, he could only wait and see and hope that his football talk hadn't bored the board too much.

The final test was an appearance before the most senior officers, fondly known as the Big Brass Hats. Bob was told to march smartly into the room, salute and say the words, 'Private Hain – Infantry to Infantry, Sir!' As he started into the room, his nerve failed him. The words came out in a quivering rush and Bob knew he wasn't sounding or looking like officer material. He was soon dismissed, one of his new companions remarking, "Gosh, yours was over in a very short time!"

CHAPTER 6

Private Hain returned to Cameron Barracks. He'd not been selected for officer training but the Board experience had been valuable and he felt privileged that he'd been chosen to have a go. The Cameron Highlanders were based here in the barracks. Bob liked to see them all dressed up in their tartan. In fact some of his fellow soldiers were so impressed that they wanted to join the regiment so that they too could wear the kilt and march against a backdrop of mist-covered moors and mountains.

But the young soldiers were here for training and a week or so later, Bob and others were dispatched to Great Yarmouth where the work involved street fighting. In empty, often derelict houses, the soldiers would hide and surprise and learn to walk on planks laid across gaps from window to window without losing their balance. Agility was important; one young soldier fell as he climbed a rope to the upper storey of a house and landed, very painfully, on his back; his training was now over. The war was in its final stages, and in Germany troops were seeking out the enemy as they sought refuge in buildings, so this kind of training was seen as urgent.

Winter was at its peak when Bob was sent from here to another coastal town, Sheringham in Norfolk. Towards the end of 1944 the weather had deteriorated and it remained bitterly cold into the new year. Outdoor training was a real endurance test but the soldiers knew better than to complain as they ran, trudged and crawled through the snow, 'attacking and defending'. With numb fingers they held their rifles into their shoulders as they practised hitting a target with live ammunition.

The spring of 1945 swept the winter away and saw Private Hain arrive back in his home county at the depot of the Dorset Regiment. Training began but was soon interrupted when farmers reported an outbreak of Foot and Mouth disease. Army personnel were called on to help, and the new recruits went out to farms where they cleaned the yards and wooden cattle sheds, scrubbing them with strong disinfectant to eliminate any trace of infection.

After the heavy bombing of Germany, now the fighting in France was going in favour of the Allies. Despite serious losses of men and materials, the Russian advance into Germany was also gaining momentum. The USA and Britain realised that Russia soon would occupy large areas of the country so, as a matter of great urgency, they gained a foothold by taking charge of West Berlin. By June 1945 Germany had surrendered to the Allies. Scenes of great rejoicing were shown on cinema newsreels, those outside Buckingham Palace being the most memorable. The war was over.

Bob was part of a unit of the 4th Dorsets and was waiting for his embarkation leave prior to departure to the Far East. However, the totally unexpected dropping of atom bombs on Nagasaki and Hiroshima swiftly changed the Allies' tactics and leave was cancelled. Instead, Bob was one of a number of men from the Dorset regiment who were sent to Gibraltar to relieve troops, many of whom were shortly to be released from the army.

Here, he was stationed at a place called La Linea, near the Spanish border. His job was to check entrants into Gibraltar and for this work he was given his first stripe. Many of the people coming through the checkpoint were Allied Troops, soldiers who had been into Spain on short-term leave, as well as some passing through on their way back from the Far East. Lance Corporal Hain enjoyed meeting them all, if only briefly. However, Gibraltar re-acquainted Bob with someone he knew much better when, back at the barracks, an old friend strode into the room. With a huge smile creasing his face and his hand outstretched, he said, "Bob Hain – I thought I heard your name mentioned!" It was Jim Burgess from Bryanston and the two had often played together in cricket matches. There was plenty to talk about and, for a while, the world seemed smaller.

The posting lasted until just before Christmas. The soldiers were looking forward to celebrating at home with their families. Bob packed his kit, included a few souvenirs from Gibraltar, but decided that the folks back in England would be most excited by a big bunch of bananas – readily available here but not seen at home for years. Most of the boys agreed with this idea and a great many bunches were loaded on board the troop ship with the soldiers. Amid much jollity, the captain prepared to leave the harbour. The big ship slowly moved away from the jetty and began to turn towards the harbour entrance. As Bob stood looking out to sea he felt, rather than heard, a thud. The captain had turned the vessel too sharply and hit the end of the jetty.

Some said he'd had too much to drink but, whatever the reason, it was quite clear that the ship and its cargo were going nowhere that day. The ship limped back to the quay, a large gaping hole in her side. The soldiers gathered up their belongings and headed back to barracks. As the days passed and the bananas began to ripen, hopes of Christmas round the fireside at home began to fade. It wasn't possible to find another ship, so the passengers had to wait until the hole in theirs had been filled with concrete and the vessel was seaworthy again.

Just after Christmas the soldiers sailed for home. By this time brown patches had appeared on the bananas and they were beginning to smell very ripe. But it wasn't important. The boys were going home and lots of celebrations were planned to mark their safe return. Once back in Durweston, Bob heard that a 'Welcome Home' dance was being planned by Nel Morgan's father, Harry, and it was to take place in Bryanston school. He was keen to go and bought a ticket for himself and one for his sister, Ena.

Over in Bryanston, Nel had heard of Bob's return and was hoping he might come to the dance. Sometimes she heard news of him at the telephone exchange where she worked because a messenger boy, who often brought letters and notes from the post office, was also a neighbour of the Hains in Durweston. Now young Ted Gillingham told her that Bob was coming to the dance and had bought a double ticket. Nel was devastated: 'Oh no – who was he bringing with him? He must have a girlfriend!'

On 18 January Mr Morgan spent the day at Bryanston school making sure everything was in order for the evening's festivities. There was a 'Welcome Home' banner to hang and the Maurice Gilbert band arrived early to set up their instruments and try out a few numbers. Nel dressed carefully. She and Bob had not met for some time and although he'd be bringing some other girl to the dance she could feel the butterflies fluttering in her tummy.

Nel met lots of friends when she walked into the hall, but as she stood laughing and chattering with them she kept one eye on the entrance doors. A taxi drew up outside. A tall young man in army uniform stepped out and opened the opposite door, giving a hand to the young lady he was escorting to the dance. Nel glanced across as the pair entered the hall. Yes – she'd know him anywhere, and oh – the relief – he was with his sister! Bob saw her straight away. If he'd thought about Nel at all it was as a schoolgirl; this was a surprise. Looking at this pretty young woman in her fashionable, flattering dress quite took his breath away for a minute. As the band struck up, he thought he ought to dance first with Ena. Nel too, was dancing with someone else but she and Bob were very aware of each other when they passed close by on the dance floor.

It didn't take long. Ena had no shortage of partners and Bob plucked up the courage to ask Nel to dance. Soon they were talking of old times and laughing about the 'Rufty Tufty' and 'Sellinger's Round' and there was a lot of 'Do you remember when …?'. But there was also plenty of catching up to do and questions about future plans. The evening finished too soon. There was so much more they wanted to say to each other and they both knew that something special had begun. Bob walked Nel home and was thrilled to find that she had no objection to a goodnight kiss. It was dark. He only had the moon and a sprinkling of stars to light his way as he walked the two miles to his house, but he wouldn't have cared if he'd had to feel his way along the hedgerows in a rainstorm. He'd found Nel again and the future looked great.

Soon, Bob realised that Ena, too, had found romance. She had been seeing an American GI for some time and he wanted to marry her. Ena knew that if she said 'yes' it would mean living in a country far from home and the family she loved. But also, she knew she loved Dick and wanted to spend her life with him. She accepted his proposal and the wedding was arranged. Bob desperately wanted to be at his sister's wedding but couldn't get leave to attend. At the time, he was spending a week or two under canvas in Tunbridge Wells and decided that it might be possible to slip away for the day, unnoticed. He had a chat with one of the other men whom he knew he could trust to cover for him.

Bob turned in early the night before the wedding because he needed to be up and away with the dawn. He couldn't sleep. Memories, questions, family and military loyalty raced around his head as he tossed and turned, while his conscience fought his will. His conscience won. Bob simply wasn't the kind of chap who could flout the rules. When his friend crept in to wake him Bob said, "Thanks for being such a good mate – but I just can't do it." So Ena's wedding went ahead in her brother's absence before she sailed away to her new life.

Soon, Nel was to become Bob's 'girl back home' because he was going with the 4th Dorsets to Germany. The battalion were now stationed in the Charlottenburg district of Berlin as part of the army of occupation, and a rather interesting phase in Bob's army career was about to begin.

Lance-Corporal Bob Hain, Berlin 1946

CHAPTER 7

There was hardly time to settle in before the army sprang a surprise on Bob. Only days after his arrival in Berlin it was decided by the 'powers that be' to set up an education section in the battalion. An education officer, Captain Andrew, was drafted in and he began by sending a questionnaire round the ranks to help him find out levels of ability. He was surprised to discover that out of the unit of 300 men only two had School Certificates, one of whom was of course Lance Corporal Bob Hain; the other was John Walling who was educated at Hele's School in Exeter. There could have been three, had not Guy Bryan from Bridport left his grammar school early to work on the family farm. Guy, however, was chosen to teach too.

Although Bob had no experience in education, Captain Andrew told him that he'd be teaching a class to read and write. The young soldier was horrified. "I can't teach," he cried, "I can't do it!" The Captain narrowed his eyes. "Oh yes, you b … well will!" was his response, and Bob knew that it wasn't his prerogative to refuse. But he was always willing to have a go at something new and tried to think positively about things. After all, the army as well as the bank had given him lots of experience in dealing with people and he'd always got on with them rather well. He might even turn out to be quite good as a teacher!

A sergeant from the RAEC (Royal Army Education Corps) was appointed to advise and gave Bob, John and Guy a short period of training. When Bob was due to begin teaching, 55 'other ranks' turned up to be educated. The RAEC sergeant looked them over and said, "I'll take 20 of them – that's an ideal class size. You can have the rest." Bob was quietly shocked to be given so many students on his first day, but he went off to the appointed room with his class of 35 and sat them down. He started the session with a friendly chat and realised that he felt quite happy with the situation. Many of the soldiers told him that they really appreciated this opportunity to learn and soon be able to write letters home.

So the teaching went well and Bob was promoted to sergeant (although this sudden advancement was not readily appreciated by some of the 'old sweat' sergeants and sergeant-majors who had had to undergo many years of service before their promotions). At first he was often asked to help with the men's letters, and some who had more difficulty in writing would ask him to write their letters for them – even to girlfriends. Sergeant Hain was enjoying his time in Berlin. Entertainers were often invited to perform for the troops and one of these was the famous Ivor Novello who thrilled them all with his own song, 'We'll Gather Lilacs'. As he sang the haunting words and played the beautiful melody, there were many wistful looks and a few moist eyes as thoughts of sweethearts back home came into the soldiers' hearts.

Those who didn't have a wife or sweetheart at home – and some of those who did – had taken to spending their evenings in the city. Here, there were plenty of young women looking for a partner, often as a diversion from the unhappiness that had spread through the defeated nation. Of course, in some cases a chance meeting would be the beginning of a happy relationship and then marriage, so for a number of German girls Britain became their new home. But the brief liaisons with the kind of girls only looking for thrills and fun meant that soon there was a rise in cases of VD (Venereal Disease) among the soldiers. This resulted in all ranks having to call in at the army company office to collect a contraceptive whenever a night out was planned to any part of town. Bob's classes were switched to the evenings in order to keep at least some of the men on the base for some of the time – like it or not.

It was decided that the education section was a success and could be transferred to other cities where British troops were stationed. Bob spent time in Hannover, Munster Lager and Brunswick. Members of the Nazi hierarchy were held in Munster Lager prior to their trials and one of Bob's non-teaching tasks here was to escort an officer prisoner to Bremen. Guards climbed in the back of a 15cwt truck with the prisoner, while Bob sat in the front with the driver, alert for any possible problems. There was variety in the day-to-day duties and time soon passed. Demobilization was drawing closer and Sergeant Hain was given his number: 61.

Attempts were made by the military to encourage people to sign on for a few more years, but although Bob had found his army service quite satisfying he was keen to get back to England, Nel, friends and family. He was interested in some information he'd received from the Civil Service, offering employment with the Metropolitan Police Service in London. An interview was arranged for him at Scotland Yard, to coincide with his next spell of leave. He travelled by bus, wondering what he would find when he arrived at the legendary police headquarters with its famous 'Whitehall 1212' phone number. A short walk from the bus stop saw Bob outside the imposing Victorian Gothic building on Victoria Embankment. He stepped inside and found the place dark and somewhat depressing. The rather precise man who interviewed him told him that it would take many years to progress within the system, with assessments and exams along the way. Bob knew straight away that he didn't want this, although he couldn't bring himself to say so. He left the building without giving an answer either way and was glad to be outside again, breathing in the cool air with its faint smell of the river.

At the back of the young man's mind were thoughts of the bank. He'd been happy there and as he stood on the corner of the street Bob made a sudden decision to visit the headquarters of the National Provincial Bank. He knew it was close by and found the building easily. As soon as he walked through the doors he felt at home. This was more like it. One of the managers noticed the tall young man and came over to him. Bob explained that he'd like to continue working at the bank and join the permanent staff. To his surprise and pleasure he was welcomed back 'with open arms'. The man told him that not everyone wanted to go back to work as a bank clerk after a more exciting life in the forces! He was introduced to a senior officer who shook him by the hand and said he would write quite soon to tell Bob which branch he would join. Bob felt happy and settled as he walked back to catch his bus.

A week or so later, he received a letter saying that he would be employed at the Dorchester branch. He accepted at once. On the day when Princess Elizabeth married Philip Mountbatten, 20 November 1947, Sergeant Bob Hain was demobbed from the army.

The Durweston boy was glad to be home and spent his time catching up with family news and seeing friends, but most of all making plans for the future with Nel. He found that he didn't miss the army and felt that that phase in his life was over. Comrades kept in touch at first, but civilian life soon begins to loosen the ties and friendships are consigned to the memory where a random conversation, a sudden smell or the sound of a voice unexpectedly brings them to mind.

It was good to have a job arranged and Bob went into Dorchester to have a look at his future workplace and meet his new colleagues. He thought he would need to take lodgings in the town so he brought this into a conversation with a couple of the staff. The bank's accountant – a man who appeared to enjoy the finer things in life – gave him the name and address of a lady in town who took in boarders. "It's very nice there," he said, "you'll be very comfortable." Bob thanked him and, before he went home, found the house in a pleasant, quiet residential street. He knocked on the rather smart front door and, when the landlady answered, told her he was looking for a room and enquired as to the cost. She smiled sweetly and said, "Four guineas a week." Since Bob would be on a starting salary of £4 weekly this wasn't good news.

He made his way home where he discussed the problem with his mother. "Well," she said, "why don't you walk round the working-class district and knock on doors?" Bob thought this wasn't a bad idea, so the next day he walked to the area of Dorchester where little terraced houses lined the streets and women in flowered aprons glanced up at him as they washed their front step or polished the letterbox with Brasso. After a few unsuccessful visits, Bob struck lucky. A Welsh lady called Mrs Foot said she'd be pleased to give him a room, breakfast and an evening meal from Monday to Friday: £3 a week. This was very acceptable and left him just enough money for the weekends and a bite to eat at lunchtimes. After Christmas, he started work and moved in with Mr and Mrs Foot.

Mrs Foot gave him good meals and a comfortable bed. However, after a time Bob discovered that he wasn't necessarily the only one using his bedroom. The house was quite small and the Foots had another tenant, a postal worker who sorted mail on the night train before getting off at Dorchester. As Bob left for work in the mornings this man was going to bed, and, as Mrs Foot eventually told him, sometimes Bob's bed. He didn't mind. Life's little refinements like your own comfortable bed had soon been knocked on the head in the army. Evening meals were a time for chatting about the day and discussing the latest news. Bob liked to listen to his landlady's Welsh lilt but occasionally he found her remarks rather quaint. Ghandi had been in the news a lot and one day it was announced on the radio that he had died. "Oh dear," said Bob, "Ghandi's dead." To which Mrs Foot replied, "Oh – he would!" Bob had no answer to this; an agreeable sort of smile had to do.

It was good to be back in a bank. Bob worked on the counter now, getting to know the Dorchester customers, and knowing that his pay would soon increase. After five months he was invited to visit Head Office again in London to discuss his permanent appointment. Here he met a Joint General Manager, a bluff Yorkshireman who fired a number of questions at him. Having finished his interrogation, the man looked at Bob and said, "Now – is there anything you want to ask or tell me?" The only thing Bob thought could be of interest was his forthcoming wedding, so he took the opportunity to tell him he was getting married the following month, August.

The JGM almost exploded in his shock and amazement. "Getting married?!... splutter ... splutter ... what on earth will you do when you get into debt?" Bob kept quite calm and cool. His teaching experience had improved his confidence and he knew he was on firm ground. His reply was careful: "Well Sir, I know that many people do overspend, irrespective of their income, but I don't. I won't get into debt."

The man stared at Bob. He saw before him someone who would not be deterred once he had made a decision. Furthermore, he saw someone whose polite self-possession would be an asset to the bank. The JGM decided that any more argument would be useless. He thrust his arm forward and, taking Bob's hand in his iron grip, said, "Welcome back!" The new member of the permanent staff was as good as his word; Bob has never broken the pledge he made that day.

CHAPTER 8

On 14 August the sun rose in a clear blue sky. In Durweston, Bob stared in the mirror as he pinned and unpinned the white carnation until it was in just the right place on the lapel of his suit. His two sisters, Betty and Kathleen, were going to be bridesmaids and tried to contain their excitement as they helped each other into the charming, deep turquoise dresses made in a soft crepe by their mother for this very special day.

In Bryanston, Harry Morgan, father of the bride, struggled with his own buttonhole while his wife pinned the wedding veil securely onto Nel's headdress. Lily Morgan, Nel's brother Cyril's wife, rushed hither and thither as she prepared the food for the wedding breakfast. Although the family ran the village shop food was rationed, but Lily had offered to organise the feast and proved to be very adept at finding extra bits and pieces stashed away in cupboards and pantries. She produced a wonderful spread. Even better, her brother was a baker and presented Bob and Nel with a beautifully iced wedding cake. Her husband Cyril, a Petty Officer in the Royal Navy, had duties of his own to plan, for he was the Best Man.

The Revd Bertie Rosson, whose prophecy had come to pass, draped his embroidered ceremonial scarf round his shoulders and smiled as he thought about the two young people he had known and guided through their childhood and beyond. He closed the vestry door and entered the church where he welcomed Bob and Cyril, and the guests who'd come early to get a good seat. The sun shone through the stained glass windows, bringing scents from the freshly-cut flowers, and very soon, the organist was playing 'Here Comes the Bride' as Nel stood in the doorway, her arm linked in Harry's. Father and daughter began the walk up the long aisle of St Martin's church.

Nel was a picture in her beautiful, white satin dress with its long train. She knew that all eyes were on her as she walked as gracefully as she could, smiling happily at people and trying to ignore the butterflies in her stomach. Just as she passed her sister-in-law, something happened. Suddenly, the dress seemed to clutch at her shoulders and round her middle so that she was stopped in her tracks. Harry, a step ahead, glanced sideways to see Nel's look of horror as she felt a waft of cool air as the fasteners on the back of her dress popped open. One of the bridesmaids had trod on her train. Lily saw what had happened. Quietly, calmly, she slid from her seat and in a matter of seconds had put the matter to rights. The bride arrived at the altar and the ceremony began. Bob thought Nel looked wonderful;

Nel shed a few tears, and suddenly, it was all over. The congregation smiled at each other and the happy couple as they passed back down the aisle and everyone thought that Bertie had led a 'lovely service'.

After the ceremony, it was time for photographs. There were only two photographers in the district and Bob had managed to book one for the event. The man turned out to be rather tetchy. While the bells pealed joyfully in the tower and the guests chatted happily in the churchyard, he took photos of the newlyweds. Once this was completed he called everyone together for a group photograph. But he seemed unhappy as he set his camera and spent some time fiddling with the mechanism. Suddenly, organising family and friends into the frame while trying to make sure there were no technical problems became too much. He shouted: "Somebody stop those b… bells!"

Bob and Bertie exchanged glances and the guests tried to cooperate. Eventually, the photographer seemed satisfied that he'd taken all the necessary pictures, but, when Bob and Nel returned from their honeymoon he told them that there was no photographic record of their big day. Unfortunately, something had 'gone wrong' with the camera. The only photo that remains

The precious wedding photograph with its inscription on the back:
'Wedding Aug 14, 1948
Bob & Nel
Mavis Lane gives horseshoe
England against Australia
All out for 52!
A memorable day'

as a momento of the wedding, apart from two tiny snaps, is one taken by a guest. It shows a little girl, Mavis Lane, giving a lucky horseshoe to Bob and his bride.

The honeymoon was spent in Newquay and London. When the reception was drawing to a close, the new husband and wife left for Templecombe where they waited for the Exeter train. On the platform, Bob sat on a wooden bench with Nel who soon noticed a slight inattention in his manner. A wireless was playing somewhere in the station and although Bob tried hard to listen to his wife's every word, one ear was fixed firmly on the Home Service. It was Test Match time and before their Exeter train arrived, England were all out for 52.

After spending the night rather grandly in an Exeter hotel's four-poster bed, Bob and Nel travelled to Newquay where tank traps still sat ominously on the beach and the weather turned bitterly cold. Here they stayed in a guest house and, as British holidaymakers have always had to, made the best of a chilly week, and enjoyed their new status as Mr and Mrs Hain. It was warmer the following week when they went to London to stay with one of Nel's family, Aunt Kate, and saw the brand new Rodgers and Hammerstein musical 'Oklahoma' while they were there. They never forgot those songs and sing them to this day while they're washing-up.

Before the wedding, Bob had approached Mrs Foot and told her he wouldn't want to be 'in digs' after he was married. "Oh no," she said, "I didn't think you'd want that!" So after the honeymoon the couple lived with Nel's parents at the shop and Post Office in Bryanston. Nel gave up her job at the telephone exchange and started working in the shop with her mother, while Bob cycled every morning to Blandford bridge where he caught the Wilts. and Dorset bus to Dorchester.

The newly marrieds enjoyed their life in the village. Bob played cricket and football, helped organise social evenings and devised little dramas, wrote verses and sang songs. Sometimes they could watch a film on a cinematograph belonging to the army. During the winter months when they weren't sitting by the fireside listening to the wireless, Bob and Nel often met up with his mother and his two sisters, Betty and Kathleen (usually known as 'Pop') and the little group devised their own entertainments. Everyone enjoyed singing and so some kind of musical game was often chosen.

One favourite game they invented used well-known tunes but brand new words. Each participant had two pieces of paper: on one they had to write the title of a song or perhaps a hymn; on the other a subject. These were shuffled and placed in two piles and each person must pick up a tune from one and a topic from the other. Then, they had to write a 'song' about the latter to fit the tune. One such masterpiece had the subject of 'Carol

Durweston Football Club in the 1940s. Bob is standing third from the left.

singing in the village' fitted to tune of the currently popular 'Buttons and Bows'. The second verse went like this:

> 'We look a sight singing Silent Night and others we have chose.
> Ask us in for heaven's sake sake 'cos you're in there by a fire that glows
> And we're out here with frozen toes.'

Or how about 'Getting up in the morning' to the tune of 'Praise my soul the King of heaven':

> 'Bless my soul it's half-past seven!
> My alarm clock didn't ring.
> Out of bed, into the bathroom,
> Grab the Cornflakes – anything.
> Listen to the weather forecast,
> Deep depression threatening!'

Both Bob and Nel loved to sing, although their musicality led them in different directions. Nel's parents were members of the Blandford Choral Society, and their daughter now joined them in performing works like Handel's 'Messiah'. While she was singing the 'Hallelujah Chorus', Bob was entertaining a different audience with popular songs of the day and comedy sketches. For he belonged to Blandford's 'Footlight Follies', a very successful variety group trained in singing and dancing by a talented lady named Joyce Carter. Bob's sister Betty sang in the chorus. He also met someone he already knew when he played opposite the photographer who'd let him down so badly on his wedding day. But by now Bob had managed to turn the disaster into an amusing tale and was never one to hold a grudge, so there was no animosity between them.

The shows were held in the cinema and always well attended and reviewed in the local newspaper. Bob liked performing so much that he decided to join the Dramatic Society too. He appeared in a variety of roles but recalls one that proved more troublesome than most and caused a great deal of amusement in the audience.

In a play called 'Worm's eye View' Bob played a Canadian air force recruit. He had to enter the stage singing a song. He knew the song well from his army days and it wasn't the kind of song to be sung in polite company. At the dress rehearsal, before an audience, the air force recruit walked onto the stage and began: 'I've been in the saddle for hours and hours; I stuck it as long as I could. I stuck it and stuck it … …' and then he was supposed to be interrupted. Bob stopped singing – but nothing happened. Silence. Aware that his fellow actors and the audience would be familiar with the words, Bob didn't quite know what to do. Seconds ticked by and helpless laughter began to work its way round the auditorium. Then the producer, a rather self-important gentleman, hissed: "Well, carry on then – I don't know this song but it goes along quite well, so carry on!" Bob realised that although the song was written into the script, the producer was the only person who didn't seem to know it and replied, "I can't! I'll be thrown out!" With some difficulty he explained the problem and then made sure that in future Maurice Gilbert would be sure to come in with his lines in good time!

CHAPTER 9

At work, Bob moved back to familiar territory when he was transferred to the Blandford branch as Cashier. He and Nel also moved home and went to live with Bob's parents in Durweston. Here, in 1952, Nel gave birth to their first child: a son, Robert Graham. Now they were a family they wanted a home of their own and moved to Home Farm, Bryanston, where they lived for a short while in a flat. But very soon they were allocated a new council house in Blandford St Mary where Cynthia Mary (Cyndy) was born in 1954.

The Hains didn't stay here for long because two years later Bob was transferred to the Newbury branch and the family left their home county of Dorset behind. They bought a brand new chalet bungalow in Montgomery Road where they lived next door to its builder, John Fuller. Many years had passed since the land had been cultivated and the ground was made up of layers of clay and gravel. But Bob was determined to make a good garden out of it and set to work.

He turned out to have green fingers. Plenty of double-digging and the good idea to add food waste to the ground began to pay dividends. It wasn't

Bob's mother Mary with Robert

Rob and Cythia (Cyndy)

too long before Nel was able to pull some carrots or a cabbage for dinner from a very useful kitchen garden. Behind this, Bob sowed a lawn where the children could play and was pleased with the results of his labours. However, it was the next residents who were to reap most of the benefits of his hard work because, after another two years, the bank sent Bob to work in Southampton.

The family moved once again, to Basset Green, Southampton. Nel's Uncle Les and Aunt Dorrie, her father's sister, also lived in the city and the two families became good friends. Les worked across the road from Bob in the Post Office; his twin boys also worked close by, both of them in the Ordnance Survey building next door. The boys, their father and Bob all went to watch the Southampton team at football on a Saturday afternoon and the family contact meant that the Hains quickly felt at home.

Sadly, Aunt Dorrie died six months after their move and Les and the boys were very glad of Bob and Nel's company at this hard time. They spent a lot of time together, enjoying meals that Nel had cooked, and Uncle Les would take his niece and her family for drives in his car. On one very exciting day the children came home from school to find a television set in the living room – a generous gift from Les.

Bob worked in Southampton for a few years but then, after a four-week training course at Godalming, he was rather pleased to hear one morning that he was to be promoted and transferred to a small county branch of the bank at Woodstock in Oxfordshire. Before lunch time, the telephone rang again for him. This time the news was a shock; his father-in-law Harry had suddenly died. Bob went home to comfort his grieving wife and his good news had to be given a back seat.

After the funeral, they all discussed the move to Oxfordshire. Woodstock would be quite a journey from Bryanston and the newly widowed Mrs Morgan, but Nel's mother understood that life moves on and knew that the change would be good for the family. A few weeks later Bob started planning the move. It was 1962.

Before starting work in his new branch, Bob took the family to Stonesfield, a village on the edge of the Blenheim Palace estate and just four miles from Woodstock. Much of the distinctive roofing slate which tops the lovely stone houses of the Cotswolds came from this village. Indeed, those who work the local allotments know that it still lives up to its name!

The Hains were in Stonesfield to look at a house called 'Four Acres', on

'Four Acres', Stonesfield, in 1962

Pond Hill. This had been the home of the man whom Bob was to replace and, thinking it would be a very nice home for them with its spacious rooms and large garden, Bob and Nel negotiated and agreed a price for it there and then. The family strolled round the village, looking at its school and two churches and noting the surprising number of good little shops. Between the buildings, they glimpsed green, rolling countryside and farmland and felt that this would be an ideal place to live – bringing them back to the village life they loved.

In no time at all, the Hains had moved into Four Acres. After passing an exam, Robert entered the first year class at Chipping Norton School. Cyndy attended Stonesfield Primary School until she joined her brother at Chipping Norton two years later. Nel busied herself in her new home and joined the WI.

At work, Bob took a liking to the Woodstock bank where he was Sub-Manager to Jack Routledge. He soon got to know his new customers and found Woodstock an interesting little town, dominated as it still is by the huge palace of Blenheim, the entrance to which is just along the road from the bank. Summertime always meant an influx of tourists which brought extra visitors, with their queries and problems, to the National Provincial branch. Bob enjoyed the extra challenges, but just as he began to feel happily settled, he found that Woodstock wouldn't be his only workplace. Very soon, he was called on for relief duties at the Cornmarket Street and Cowley Road branches in Oxford, and the Bank in Bicester. This was followed by more settled work at the Chipping Norton branch. He was getting to know Oxfordshire rather well.

Bob, Nel and the two children all attended the parish church of St James the Great, and one Sunday morning a lady in the congregation found her thoughts wandering away from the sermon and settling on the father of the new family sitting opposite her. Marjorie Woodward was the secretary of Stonesfield Youth Club and had a bit of a problem. Marjorie had started the club the previous year, 1961, but now its voluntary leader, Brian Morris, was going to have to leave and she needed a replacement. As she looked at Bob, she recalled that he'd talked about being a Boy Scout, dealing with people in the bank and teaching in the army. Well, wouldn't he be the ideal person? Marjorie decided to ask him after the service and turned the pages to find the next hymn.

Bob was surprised to be considered for the job, being so new to the village, but not displeased. He felt he might have the kind of skills the work would need and decided to give it a try. After all, he wouldn't be on his own; there was a good team of Council youth workers based in Oxford and Witney whom he could call on for advice at any time. Yes, he'd have a go.

CHAPTER 10

A few days later, Bob walked round the corner to the club's HQ – the old village hall which sat opposite the Police House in Woodstock Road. He got on well with the young people and began to look at their present activities and plan what he could add to them. Eventually, there was table tennis, darts for both boys and girls, chess and draughts, drama and public speaking. Bob particularly enjoyed producing the annual one-act play. The young actors would travel over to the Pegasus theatre in Cowley, Oxford where their play formed part of a drama festival for young people. Each club would perform their play which was then assessed by a professional judge.

Under Bob's guidance and encouragement a number of the teenagers became sufficiently confident to enter an annual public-speaking competition. An entry usually involved three people: one to introduce the speaker and the subject, one to give the speech and one to comment afterwards. Then each trio's efforts were judged by an official.

Indoor football and summer rounders, cricket and athletics brought the club in contact with others when matches were arranged by Joyce Trafford, a very helpful youth worker from Witney. This meant that extra help was needed from local volunteers and that Bob must organise transport and find referees and umpires. Frank Hall, whose son Stephen and daughter Rosemary were keen club members, and was a person always ready to lend a hand, was one who helped drive the teams to their fixtures. (Bob enjoyed football himself and occasionally played in goal for the Stonesfield second team.)

Another valuable helper was Trevor Coles, the village policeman. PC Coles lived in the Police House across the road, so was usually on hand if any little disciplinary problems arose – as they did one evening when some lads from Woodstock came over for a Youth Club dance and started a fight. When Trevor was called and appeared in the doorway, boys sprang apart and tried to look as if butter wouldn't melt in their mouths. In those days a village Bobby was a person to be treated with respect, and peace was restored without delay.

Bob ran the Youth Club for more than four years and left a generation of village teenagers with good memories of happy times. There was the excitement of an all-night hike around West Oxfordshire to raise money for Oxfam, and a relay race around the area – quite possible in those days when there was much less traffic. Added to these was the memorable introduction of folk dancing.

This latter caused a bit of a rebellion in the ranks when it was first suggested. One boy told their leader, "You're goin' to ruin this club Mr 'ain." But, although there'd been a lot of arguing and grumbling, Bob was pleased when, towards the end of one evening meeting one of the boys said, "All right, let's have a go at this folk dancing then." He was even more pleased when, having decided that they rather liked this new activity, all the youngsters from the Griffin family turned up in matching outfits, ready to face any competition Bob might produce for them. And he did. Each year the club sent a team to the District Youth Folk Dance competition at Carterton where they had a degree of success.

But at work, things were not so good. The bank was having difficulties in staffing the London branches and Bob had to spend time working in Victoria Street, Belgravia and King's Road, Chelsea. It meant staying in hotels and only coming home for weekends. He didn't care for this at all and neither would he be able to continue leading the Youth Club if he was spending so much time away. But just at the right moment, along came Pat Gibbs from nearby Wootton. Pat took over from Bob as leader and Bob became the helper. The club was to remain active for 38 years.

During that time, an enthusiastic, red-haired lady known as Ginge West brought another skill to the club. Ginge was a very skilful swimmer and

Martin Pauling hands over the cheque to buy a hospital bed

taught life-saving techniques to the members. She was their popular leader for ten years. During her leadership, Bob continued to support new ideas and initiatives. The young members were always happy to try something new and keen to raise money for a good cause – although a sponsored 24-hour fast was testing. To make sure they had no access to food, they were locked in the village hall for the length of the fast, by which time they were quite desperate for their mothers' cooking! The money was presented to the Churchill Hospital to buy a bed for their Neurology Unit, and was handed over by Martin Pauling who raised the largest amount.

Nel loved her new village but thought the one thing it lacked was a good choir. There was an opportunity to play an instrument in the very successful Stonesfield Silver Band but Nel had always loved to use her voice and sing. And it wasn't too long before she was able to. When she was chatting with one of her new friends she heard the news that a conductor, Charles Common, had moved into the village. This was just what she wanted to hear. Nel encouraged people to come to a meeting and in 1963 twelve ladies formed the new Stonesfield Choral Society.

From this gentle beginning, the Society grew into a mixed choir of 40 members who performed all kinds of music from mediaeval to modern and a good carol concert at Christmas, in venues as different as the village hall and the Sheldonian Theatre. The Choral Society thrived for the next 25 years until the number of members declined and those who still wanted to sing were drawn away by the nearby and thriving Woodstock Choral Society. Other conductors had succeeded Charles Common but Nel and Bob remained his good friends. When Charles and his wife moved up to the north of Scotland, the Hains kept in touch and went to visit them in their new home.

It was 1967 and his children were at an age when Bob felt that they needed both parents to guide and care for them. He decided to talk to his bank's Staff Manager and made an appointment to talk about the relief work. The Manager understood his point of view and, after a good discussion, it was agreed that Bob would only be employed in local branches so that he could continue living at home. Bob and Nel decided that this called for a celebration, so during his final week in London, at Hyde Park, Nel came to join him. They went to see 'The Mousetrap', the play which had been running since 1952, the year of their son's birth. But never did they dream that it would still be possible to see it in 2013!

CHAPTER 11

Bob liked the theatre and had enjoyed his time in the Footlight Follies and the drama group. So on arrival in Stonesfield he wasted no time in joining the Amateur Dramatic Society. At that time the number of actors was quite small and a play had to be chosen more for its correct number of male and female roles than for its content. In 1966, a man called Dan Short, who was a very good technician, revived the society, giving it a new start as the Stonesfield Players.

Bob took leading parts in a number of plays, including the challenging role of Creon in 'Antigone' with his daughter Cyndy prompting from the wings. It was a very dramatic play and when it was over he felt emotionally 'wrung out'.

But he thoroughly enjoyed playing a nasty, uncouth character in 'A Letter from the General'. In this play he had to pretend to hit one of the female actors and practised smacking his hand as he raised his arm until he felt the action would look and sound convincing. It worked. As Bob's fist struck his other hand with a sharp 'thwack!' a gasp went up from the audience. He'd been told that people watching him needed to see him as a real villain, and it appeared he was successful. His neighbour, a lady who was on very friendly terms with Bob and Nel, was in the audience with her husband. She tackled Bob the next day. "I didn't know you were like that,"

Bob and Diana Dawe in a Stonesfield Players' production of Wanted: One Body.

she told him. "Now I've seen another side of you I didn't know you had." "But it's called 'acting'!" replied Bob. "Oh no, it wasn't," insisted the woman and refused to be persuaded. They remained friends; whether or not she felt slightly wary of him now Bob never knew.

The players put on a good mixture of works. The audience, often seeing a friend or neighbour perform on the stage, roared with laughter at the comedies, tried to guess the ending of a mystery and wiped away the odd tear in a tragedy. But of course, as with all amateur dramatic societies, there were those times when things didn't quite work out and little incidents became part of a group's history.

There was the time when Bob moved a table and its legs fell off, causing great hilarity. Once, while playing a serious part, his false moustache started to slip sideways. Turning his back slightly, he tried more than once to press it firmly onto his upper lip. The audience began to sense a possible diversion and watched with interest. As he spoke Bob felt the moustache creeping over his mouth. Again he lifted his arm as casually as he could and attempted another repair. It was no good; as Bob uttered the next line the moustache drifted down to the floor. The drama of the play was forgotten as gusts of laughter swept around the hall. Everyone knew that, for a long time to come, neighbourly conversations would be opened with the words: "Do you remember when Bob Hain's moustache fell off in that play?"!

Folk dancing in Leiden in 1981. Bob and Nel are in the foreground

In 1971 Bob and Nel smiled at the news of something that reminded them of their happy, dancing schooldays. Stonesfield was to have a Folk Dance Club. From now on, every Wednesday evening saw them walking round to the new village hall where they learned new dances and met new friends. Not only did dancers come from outside the village, but before too long, from outside the county. The club was a great success and Stonesfield soon had an annual Folk Festival as well as its six Saturday evening dances.

Later on, in 1980, the group were very pleased to welcome folk dancers from Oxford's Dutch twin town, Leiden. Most of the visitors were considerably younger than their English counterparts but they all had a wonderful time together. Bob and Nel, along with the rest of the Stonesfield members, were delighted to open their home to some of the young people. The club could hardly wait until the following year when they themselves paid a return visit to Holland to dance again with their Leiden friends.

During the 1950s the village had explored the possibility of having a playing field. One of the farmers, Bernard Hunt, had offered a field to the Playing Fields Committee for a reasonable price, with an extra acre thrown in at no cost, but it still took a rather apathetic village more than a decade to raise the purchase price. The playing field was officially opened at the village fete in 1964, by the actor Bob Arnold, who played Tom Forrest in 'The Archers'. The old Committee was disbanded and replaced by a Management Committee with representatives from many of the village organisations.

Only a year afterwards, some of these people began to think about a new village hall. The old one, where Bob ran the Youth Club and Nel attended the WI, had been built from three wooden huts, no longer needed by the British army. So by now, the building was in a sorry state. A village meeting was held in the dusty old hall and although it was obvious to all that its life was limited, there was opposition to a new one. Brian Hodgson, whose love and concern for Stonesfield and village life led him to be a County Councillor, spoke for the project with great enthusiasm. Eventually, the motion succeeded by just 19 votes. The fund-raising could start in earnest.

Bob joined the funding committee, under the chairmanship of Len Willey – a man who soon had the £s rolling in. All kinds of daytime and evening events were organised, from the usual Whist Drives and dances to the more imaginative like the Miss Stonesfield Contest. Committee members clocked up the miles on Mondays as they walked round the village collecting a shilling (5p) from households for entry into the weekly draw.

A large group of villagers walked as many as 20 miles on Whit Monday in 1968. The road walk was an annual fund-raising event and this year the destination was Swinbrook. More than 85 people had been promised a total of £250 in sponsorship by their friends and neighbours. Brian Hodgson 'fired the starting pistol' and it was a happy, chattering crowd that set off on

The walk to Swinbrook, Whit Monday 1968

a fine spring morning. Busy birds twittered as they fed their new families and the scents of the blossoming hedgerows softened the clean spring air. From the youngest child to the most elderly, their eager steps were fuelled by the promise of a good lunch on arrival at Swinbrook village hall. A team of helpers had driven over during the morning laden with food and drink which was all ready and waiting by the time the first walkers burst triumphantly through the doors.

Not every walker managed the whole 20 miles, especially those whose legs were just too little or plagued with a bit of arthritis, but 60 people completed the whole course. The success of the event was not just in the satisfaction of raising money, but in the benefits to the community as the walk gave people precious time to form new friendships and revive old ones. All the events strengthened the community as people worked towards the same goal and eventually, after more than five years of fund-raising, the new hall was opened. It had cost £24,000. A government grant had provided £10,000 but the proud villagers had raised the rest.

The architect, Andrew Allen, had lived in the village and rang Bob one day saying, "I've got an idea – I'll let you know tomorrow when we meet." But Bob never learned of the idea because very sadly the man died that night. Nevertheless, the builders, Pether & Sons of Burford, had done an excellent job and Stonesfield was rightly proud of its new hall.

CHAPTER 12

The British Tourist Board had been thinking. Visitors flocked to see the sights of London; people poured into Oxford, Stratford-upon-Avon, Edinburgh and York; Longleat, Windsor Castle and Stonehenge were always busy. But there was an important aspect of Britain that wasn't always appreciated – that of its beautiful villages and their special way of life.

Members of the Board considered this for some time, finally coming up with an idea in 1975 that they hoped would raise the profile of rural communities with their history, traditions and wealth of skills and talents. It was decided to hold a series of festivals in all parts of the British Isles. They'd be spread over the summer months and the title of the event was to be 'Festival of Villages, Summer '75'. Of course, it would only be a few lucky villages that were chosen as venues, but here Stonesfield had a distinct advantage.

Quite recently, a man with a mop of dark hair, a beard and enormous enthusiasm had moved into the village. His name was Simon Watson and by coincidence, he was a good friend of Leonard Lickorish who had the job of organising the festivals for the Tourist Board. After a short period of negotiation and persuasion, Simon brought the news that Stonesfield was to represent the Cotswold region and its festival, held over the Whitsun bank holiday, had been chosen to be the very first one. It was up to the villagers to show what they could do; they didn't want those following on to be learning from Stonesfield's mistakes!

A committee was needed, and formed quickly. Bob, who loved events that brought people together, was pleased to be invited to be part of it. After a meeting in London, planning began in earnest. Because it would be a long weekend, three full days of activities were needed. The Stonesfield Players, the Folk Dance Club and a folk music group, the Junior Silver Band, Morris dancers and crafts people all agreed to join in. One of the old slate mines, at Spratt's Farm, would be open, as would nearby Combe Mill, with its old steam beam engine. Nel was busily planning refreshments with the W.I. who would provide them in a marquee on the village playing field.

Simon was also planning. He was a big, positive thinker and was convinced that festival-goers would flock to the village. Bob arrived home one day to find that his garage was stacked almost to the roof with crates of soft drinks ordered by Simon to meet the needs of the crowds. A row of portable toilets had been ordered and erected and, through his connections, Simon even managed to arrange extra trains to run from London to nearby

Stonesfield Folk Dance Club open the Village Festival in 1975

stations. A sense of excitement and expectation filled the air as the weekend approached.

May 24 dawned bright and clear and the festival was opened by the Marquis of Tavistock and his wife Henrietta Tiarks, one of the leading debutantes of the time and a great beauty. Most of the villagers were there and bought a programme which covered the weekend's events. Much of the entertainment took place in a barn belonging to Bernard Hunt and was just a few doors away from Bob and Nel's house. Those who were there enjoyed the three-day weekend and all agreed it was a great time. But they were mostly local people. Very few visitors came from outside Stonesfield and there was little use for the extra trains and toilets after all. Fortunately, the fizzy drinks were delivered on a sale or return basis so Bob was able to send a number of crates back without cost.

But whilst the festival was not a profitable venture it had nevertheless been jolly good fun and a good start to the series. Festivals continued throughout the summer with the final one, number 16, being held in Braemar, Scotland in September.

After a decade had passed, the rector of St James the Great, Canon John Grimwade, thought, 'Wouldn't it be a good idea to hold another festival?' Bob and Nel regularly attended the village church, Bob becoming a Reader and then a Church Warden. They admired John and supported his idea enthusiastically. It was 1986 and this time the church would organise the festival along with the Methodist chapel – with a great peal of bells at the beginning and end. John wasn't particularly interested in raising money but wanted people to have a thoroughly enjoyable time.

Bob was involved with the planning again, with Judy Poore as chairman. Local people opened their gardens; there were singers, musicians, dancers and mummers to entertain; a barbecue and teas to enjoy; two flower festivals and demonstrations of craft-work to admire. At the end of day three, the church bells rang out to signify the end of a very successful time which had been so well-organised and supported that a profit of over £2,000 was divided between three charities. And many of the village people continued to wear their special festival T-shirts until they were quite threadbare.

So for the Hains village life continued on its sociable, rural way with the annual cycle of events changing only slightly as one or two of the older people passed on and some with fresh ideas joined the community.

A man by the name of Jimmy French, husband of the District Nurse, really wanted Stonesfield to have its own Tennis Club. There had been a Club in the village in 1922 until the outbreak of the second World War and again for a short time in the early 60s, but in 1978 there was no real opportunity

The 1986 Festival T-shirts: Bob with Canon John Grimwade (centre) and Richard Chancellor

Fencing the new tennis courts in 1982

to play. Jimmy thought that since Bob Hain was by now the chairman of the Village Hall Committee he'd be the ideal person to approach. So they held a few meetings and then Bob, who was never a tennis player, agreed to be chairman of the new Stonesfield Tennis Club.

If there was to be a Tennis Club there would have to be courts to play on and two hard courts would cost £8,500. Fund-raising must begin again! The tried and tested weekly draw was re-introduced, along with dances and some fresh events in the new hall. By 1981 the money was there and work could begin on land adjoining the football field. The only small problem was that this area of land wasn't quite big enough. The court needed to be a foot or two larger than the space available.

Bob Hain and Mike Smith went over to the farm to see Bernard Hunt. Their idea was to buy this small extra section of land – if he would sell it. Bernard wouldn't hear of this. No, he wouldn't sell it to them – he'd give it. "Just move the fence," he said, "put it where you want it!" His generosity meant that work could start straight away, most of it, after the initial digging out and surfacing, done by Bob, Mike and their group of volunteers. The courts were soon in regular use and in 1998 a third one was built, and the club members now played in league competitions.

CHAPTER 13

Rob and Cyndy Hain had had a happy childhood, full of interest. As teenagers, they tolerated their parents' busy lives with either a faintly amused smile or an irritated frown, depending on the effect the latest venture was having on the family. What they could always depend upon was plenty of visitors coming and going in Four Acres and it was really quite interesting, having an open house. Who would turn up next?

But, all too soon, they had grown up and Cyndy, now working at Blackwell's Children's Bookshop, had left the family home and moved to Oxford where she had digs with a Miss Fison in the Woodstock Road. The house was always full of music because Miss Fison taught people to play the piano. Two of her students were Anglican priests-in-training from St Stephen's House and one day the teacher had arranged a musical evening for them and a few others. Miss Fison wanted Cyndy to be there too. But Cyndy had been visiting her parents in Stonesfield and the weather was dreadful. It was raining hard and Nel didn't want her to go out. But their daughter was keen to go and eventually Bob agreed to drive her into Oxford.

Arriving at the house, Cyndy entered the music room just as the evening began. One of the young priests-to-be, Colin, sat at the piano and began to play. Cyndy stood with the group just behind him and joined in as they started to sing. Colin pricked up his ears – one of those girls had a particularly lovely, clear voice. He wanted to know whose it was and could hardly wait for the end of the piece so that he could turn round and find out. When he realised it was Cyndy who sang so well he struck up a conversation that was the beginning of a romance. The two became inseparable and before long they were married in Cyndy's parish church of St James the Great. Her brother Rob, along with all the guests and many of the villagers, thought the couple looked very happy and just right for each other. In fact the wedding had started Rob thinking, maybe it was time for him to get married too? He'd been courting a friend of Cyndy's for some time now, so why wait?

Rob and Veronica were married soon afterwards, but it wasn't a marriage made in heaven. Sadly, within a month it was all over and the couple were divorced. Bob and Nel felt rather worried about Rob. Not only had he had a disastrous relationship but he was also in a rather dead-end job which gave him little satisfaction. Then he bought a motorbike. This gave him a new interest and some good rides out with friends but one day, when Bob was helping out at Woodstock Youth Club with a play, the phone rang. There had been an accident and Rob was badly hurt. The accident resulted in Rob's being on sick leave for a year.

When his son was fit again, Bob sought advice from a villager, Norman Rotherham, who was a schools' career advisor. This man agreed to have a word with Rob and asked him directly, "What do you really want to do?" Rob replied, "I want to be an artist." Norman took him seriously and found him a place at Banbury College. The young man was very happy with this. He found accommodation in Banbury and got stuck in. Now that he was doing something he loved he worked very hard, and before long qualified to study at Loughborough University. While there, he met a Scottish girl, Maggie, and fell in love. They were married in Selkirk, near Maggie's home, and Rob opened up a studio. The children arrived; Harriet, Philippa and Charlotte were followed by Alexander who was also destined to become an artist. He works with his father in their studio in Selkirk.

Cyndy and Colin's first home, and his first parish, was at Boldon Colliery near Newcastle-on-Tyne. This was followed by three years by the sea at Weymouth before he took over the parish at Grimethorpe Colliery in Yorkshire, home of the famous Band. By now they had two growing boys, Stephen and Michael, and Bob and Nel were very pleased to hear that both lads had joined the Grimethorpe Colliery Junior Band.

During the miners' strikes in the mid-eighties, Colin was very concerned for the families in his parish, so many of whom were angry and worried. At work, Bob went down to the dining room one day, glanced at the television screen and saw his son-in-law. Colin was being interviewed and his questioner was hoping that the priest would come down on one side or the other. But Colin was having none of it. He said, "I'm not here to make judgements – I'm here for reconciliation." Bob was very proud of him.

Eventually, Colin left the Church of England and became a Roman Catholic priest. Stephen decided to teach, but Michael followed in his father's footsteps and is also a Roman Catholic priest. Colin and Cyndy live in Ashby-de-la-Zouch.

CHAPTER 14

It was the beginning of a new decade, the 1980s. Nel was happily settled in her working life where she had a position in the office of the Marlborough School, Woodstock. But Bob's career was about to lead him along a totally unexpected but new and exciting path.

Some years previously the National Provincial Bank had taken over the Westminster Bank to become National Westminster, or NatWest. By now, banking methods had shifted from hand-written ledgers and statements, and mechanisation was taking over. Older staff members who were mostly involved in book-keeping saw their work becoming obsolete as the new machines were installed in branches, whereas younger employees were pleased to be part of the progress and were quick to learn the new ways.

Every three months, Bob went to Oxford to attend a sub-managers' meeting and when he arrived one morning he was introduced to a woman from Head Office. She was visiting areas to tell everyone about an interesting new scheme set up by the bank. The idea was that employees who felt that they were too old to learn the skills required by the new systems, or indeed whose own skills were no longer needed, could instead become involved in charity work of their own choosing – and the great thing about it was that they would still be paid by the bank and have their pension rights preserved. Bob and his colleagues would be eligible to apply for this work.

The sub-managers listened intently. Some were not all that impressed by the scheme. Any chance of promotion would disappear and they'd miss the 'cut and thrust' of the banking world if they agreed to this plan. This was exactly what Bob wouldn't miss. The thing he liked best about banking was dealing with and helping people, and if he could find a charity that would be pleased to have him he'd be in an ideal job. Using his skills to improve people's lives and getting paid for it – what an opportunity! He knew he was sitting there with a smile on his face and could hardly wait to get home and tell Nel. Bob couldn't quite envisage the future but he was certainly looking forward to it.

As Bob expected, Nel was thrilled by the news and felt that perhaps she too would be able to play a part in his new venture. Things moved quickly. Bob was invited to work for the Leonard Cheshire Foundation, a charity that supports people with disabilities both in the UK and many other countries. He was offered the position of Appeal Organiser at one of the residential homes, near Banbury. The home was in need of an extension and a huge sum of money was required to fund the new building. Bob's task would be to talk to as many people as possible and encourage them or their organisation to donate to this cause. He visited the home, met with staff and residents and liked what he saw. He accepted without hesitation and threw himself into the work with enthusiasm.

Very quickly, Bob found that he had a real aptitude for persuading people to part with their money, the reason being that he was sincere and his audience readily became convinced of the integrity of his request. The job meant lots of travelling and visiting because he could be invited to speak at meetings anywhere in the country. 'Round Table' groups, 'Inner Wheel' groups, church groups and the like sent requests to Bob and he was pleased to visit them, often accompanied by Nel. At Windermere they stayed in a tailor's shop and after church on Sunday, where the man's wife was in the choir, discovered the sparkling beauty of the lake as they strolled along its shores. The couple went to Scotland on a number of occasions and following one meeting, were thrilled when their hosts took them out to have a go at Scottish folk dancing, after which they were put to bed in true Scottish style – with a whisky!

Money rolled in steadily. It didn't take too long before the target was reached and the building work could begin in earnest. Bob was on the committee of the Leonard Cheshire Foundation and regularly drove up to London to attend meetings. Leonard himself attended these meetings, although he was a very busy man and usually left as soon as he'd said his piece. As Appeal Organiser, Bob always gave a report about all the talks he'd been giving – not quite realising how much his work was being noted and appreciated.

Now, Bob found he had time to turn his attention to another aspect of the charity's work, that of supplying their overseas homes with essential equipment. This really interested him and in 1988 he became the administrator for the Cheshire Homes Aids to the Disabled section: CHAD. Cheshire homes had been established in many overseas countries by now and all of them needed wheelchairs, crutches and zimmers, artificial limbs – in fact anything that would help their residents.

Until now, all the equipment sent abroad had been purchased, but after a bit of research Bob discovered that there was a large store of unwanted apparatus scattered around the country. If only he had a large vehicle, he thought, he could pick them up. So although he had no experience of driving a lorry, he wasted no time in hiring one. It wasn't too big – in fact when it was parked between the great towering vehicles that sat outside some of the places he visited (sometimes at a rather jaunty angle) Bob thought it looked faintly comical. But he soon got used to driving it and three trips up to the DHSS store in Heywood, Lancashire yielded 100 wheelchairs. Some were

Wheelchairs in the drive at Four Acres, 1991

unused but many were in need of some repairs, so Bob got out his tools and one by one, made them ready for dispatch.

Nearer to home, he found an organisation, allied to the NHS, that took in and repaired old wheelchairs. Some of these, having been scrutinised, were considered unfit for repair and wouldn't be re-issued; they were, however, good enough for Bob. With a bit of extra work they could be made serviceable for sending abroad. So most Saturday mornings Bob and Nel drove separate cars into Oxford to pick up as many chairs as they were able to fit inside their vehicles – five or six for Bob, but eight in Nel's case as her red Austin estate was the bigger car. The need was great, but under Bob's direction the stocks gradually increased.

Even so, CHAD wanted more. On one of his regular visits to Dorset with Nel, Bob was sitting chatting with his brother-in-law, Gordon Davies. He was talking about the frequent requests for help and the constant round of obtaining, mending and supplying. Gordon listened carefully and then offered to help. His mechanical knowledge was first-class and he saw no problems with picking up and returning the wheelchairs. Bob accepted his offer immediately. Gordon would be able to do the repair work quicker than he could, so they could send even more equipment overseas. True to his word, Gordon travelled over 200 miles every week to and from Oxfordshire in a hired van, fetching broken wheelchairs and returning those he'd mended.

The next challenge was getting the cargo to its destination. Bob was so pleased when he found that nearly all of the airlines were willing to help out. He only had to mention the name 'Leonard Cheshire' to find that it was a passport to free shipping. All he had to do was get the goods to Heathrow. So once again he hired a truck and, after a bit of trial and error, found the best way of loading the equipment so that the lorry would be stable and as full as possible. Then, he drove it down to Heathrow Airport to be loaded on to a transport plane. It was exciting to realise that the destinations would be as far-flung as Zimbabwe, Zambia, Nigeria, Sierra Leone, Kenya and South Africa.

Back in Stonesfield, friends and neighbours had heard about the charity and would turn up at Four Acres' door with clothing and gifts of cash for CHAD. Both Stonesfield and neighbouring Combe W.I. groups regularly held events such as carol concerts to raise money for this cause that seemed to touch people's hearts. Down in Dorset, Gordon also found much goodwill, especially from people who donated used wheelchairs. One day, Bob was talking about the transport situation to his good friend and neighbour, Squadron Leader Frank Huddleston. Frank thought for a minute and then said, "Well, that shouldn't be a problem…" and arranged for the RAF to help out too. So it wasn't long before more trips were arranged to homes in Sri Lanka, Indonesia, Swaziland and Cyprus. One thing leads to another and soon the army were helping, with distribution from the container port at Marcham, near Southampton. Soon, supplies were sailing or winging their way to all parts of the world, to 50 countries in all continents except North America.

CHAPTER 15

One morning, just after Bob arrived at his office the telephone rang. It was a call from Lady Gill Braithwaite who said that her husband was the British Ambassador in Moscow. She said, "You know, there's a great need in Russia for wheelchairs and similar equipment – we've had a request." Bob said he was sure he could help but was interested to find out how Lady Braithwaite had come to ring him. "Well," she said, "I tried the British Legion but they said they didn't do this kind of thing. So I tried the Red Cross and they said they didn't do it either, but they knew a man who did!"

Bob managed to find fifty good wheelchairs and loaded them onto the truck. He drove them to Heathrow from where British Airways flew them, free of charge, to Moscow. The ambassador's wife was absolutely delighted to hear that the chairs had arrived and could hardly wait to arrange their distribution herself.

The Head of Home in Banbury lived in a little house near the main gate. She was a kind, spirited lady called Betty Paget-Clarke, who, at Bob's suggestion, also became Chairman of the Leonard Cheshire Foundation's committee. Betty came to the charity having been a dancer with a very elite troupe in Paris. She told Bob that discipline in the troupe was far tighter than that of the British army! Her husband was a pilot and Betty had flown with him to the Middle East as his navigator; she was an interesting person with unusual talents.

One day, Betty popped her head into the room where Bob and his colleagues were working and asked them to come and meet some people. Out in the hall of the Home, a group of military-looking Americans were waiting. The party was from the USAF base in Upper Heyford, a base which was due to close quite soon, and Betty had invited the airmen to come and see the Home before they left. While they were looking around, Bob found himself next to someone who described herself as secretary of the group. Never one to miss an opportunity, Bob asked her what would happen to the equipment at the base when they all left. The woman couldn't give a definite answer but promised to find out for him. Sure enough, a letter arrived only a few days later. It looked very official and stated rather stiffly that all unused equipment would be passed to 'another theatre'. Bob shrugged his shoulders but thought it had been worth a try.

A few days later, a lorry trundled up the drive of the Cheshire Home. Bob, glancing out of the window, thought he recognised the driver. He went outside with Betty and realised that the man in the cab was Bill Williams, a driver at the USAF base and a great friend of the Cheshire Home. "Where can I off-load the cargo then?" he called. The 'cargo' was a three-ton load of brand new sheets and bedding! This was wonderful. Bill said he'd been able to convince his employers at the base that the linen could be of real use in Cheshire Homes throughout the world. Bob thanked him gratefully and assured him that he'd set about the distribution straight away so that Bill could tell them at Upper Heyford that things would indeed be exactly as he'd said.

By 1982, the new wing of the Banbury home was at last complete. The residents and staff were delighted with it and Betty decided that there must be a Grand Opening Ceremony. They needed someone special to 'cut the ribbon' and she discussed the possibilities with Leonard Cheshire. Leonard had already been thinking about this and told Betty of his choice, the legendary Group Captain Sir Douglas Bader. Oh my word! Wouldn't that be wonderful? To entertain this man, who was a legend in his own lifetime, and had himself done so much for disabled people, in their Home would really be the best they could imagine.

Douglas Bader had joined the RAF in 1928 and was commissioned in 1930. He was a fearless pilot but crashed whilst attempting aerobatics the following year and lost both his legs. He almost died, but slowly recovered and was fitted with artificial legs. All he wanted to do was to fly again and eventually managed to persuade the RAF to let him serve in the Second World War in 1939. His bravery was second to none and accounts of his heroic victories over German aircraft are many. In 1941 he was promoted to Wing Commander and had his initials painted on the side of his own Spitfire. In August of that year he bailed out of his aircraft after it was attacked, but in doing so, his right prosthetic leg was damaged beyond repair.

Although he was captured and became a prisoner of war, his German guards treated Douglas with great respect. The British were notified of his damaged leg and it was arranged that the RAF would be given safe passage in order to drop off a new one. So a brand new artificial right leg drifted to the ground by parachute near St Omer Luftwaffe base in France.

After the leg was fitted, Douglas Bader planned his escape from the hospital. This was accomplished by the time-honoured method of tying sheets together and clambering down. His escape was the first of quite a number; in fact his German captors became so irritated by him that they threatened to take away his legs. Finally, in 1942, he was sent to Colditz Castle where escape was almost impossible and where he remained until the Americans liberated it in 1945.

And this was the man who would open the Home's new wing. Residents and staff looked forward to the Grand Opening with great anticipation. When the day finally came Douglas Bader arrived with his wife and was warmly welcomed by Betty. As well as the people who lived and worked at the home there were at least a hundred guests. Douglas was introduced to a number of these and then the afternoon programme began.

A picture of an aeroplane had been hung on the wall below the commemorative plaque which was covered by a small curtain. When the time came for him to pull the curtain cord, Douglas laughed and said that the last time he'd done something similar, the curtain had drawn back to reveal a picture of a naked lady – a prank organised by some of his air force friends. No such naughtiness here! After the opening ceremony, the guest of honour toured the new wing, spoke with residents and was interested to hear from Bob how the money for the building had been raised.

He was particularly taken by a pair of walking boots which were fixed to a plinth. These belonged to a local 'Rotarian' who had completed a long, sponsored walk for the charity. A little card attached to the laces told how much money had been raised. Douglas picked up the boots, looked at Bob and said, "Now – I'm going to say a few words and then call upon everyone present to put some cash into these!" After which he handed Bob the boots, telling him, "I want you to stand right here and don't let the b… s go past without putting something in!" For some time he stood near to Bob and the boots, watching each person as they passed by. He wasn't disappointed; nobody dared to ignore his request and a good sum of money was donated throughout the afternoon.

It had been a great success. Douglas Bader was thanked by the Head of Home and left for his own home with his wife. Sadly, because of a heart condition that was worsening, he died less than a month later.

In July 1992 Leonard Cheshire, Lord Cheshire of Woodhall, also died. The news was received with great sadness all over the world. In her speech on Christmas Day of that year, the Queen talked of his work and his unfailing Christian dedication to helping others. But although Leonard would be greatly missed, his charity was so firmly established and its workers so dedicated that there was no doubt over its continuing work.

CHAPTER 16

A lady called Penny Mharapara had come from Zimbabwe for nursing training at a London hospital. Her task would be to visit Cheshire Homes in Zimbabwe, Zambia and other parts of Southern Africa and pass on her skills to the staff. Bob got to know Penny and found her to be a very reliable lady and overseas contact. While she was in England she asked the charity to ask for help for the Homes in Harare. Bob was the person she needed to see, so she travelled to Oxfordshire and stayed with him and Nel in Stonesfield while plans and arrangements were made. They all enjoyed being together and Penny's talk of Zimbabwe began to give Bob the beginnings of an idea: perhaps he and Nel could pay a return visit to Penny and see the work of the charity in Harare? It was certainly something to consider.

Meanwhile, he got down to finding the badly needed supplies. He gathered a large number of sheets and wheelchairs together but also had a good collection of items including crutches and walking frames which had been donated by a retailer. The lorry was satisfyingly full when Bob drove it to Heathrow. The equipment was received with much excitement in Harare and another letter of thanks and appreciation joined the growing pile in Bob's office.

He decided that he and his wife must go to Zimbabwe. Gordon and his wife, Bob's sister Kathy, thought they would like to go too. So in 1995 the flights were booked, the suitcases were packed and four excited people took to the skies. They had asked to stay in the Masterton Cheshire Home for a number of days so that they could see at first hand what it was like for the residents there.

The Hains found the Home quite bleak. A bed was the only piece of furniture in the rooms. But the staff were caring, the residents grateful and Bob and Nel, Gordon and Kathy were glad to have been there before moving on to the greater comfort of a hotel in the city. Penny took the four visitors to see other projects based elsewhere in Harare; homes for children, homes for mothers and babies who were otherwise alone; projects which had such a long way to go but were led by people with positivity and optimism. It was good to see how the donated equipment had been used and what else might be needed. Where Penny was involved in organising hospital work, she made sure that residents were actively engaged in carrying out minor repairs to the equipment they used and not just sitting around awaiting attention.

CHESHIRE HOMES NAMIBIA

for children with physical disabilities

Bob Hain
Oxfordshire Cheshire Home
Greenhill House
Twyford, Banbury
Oxon, OX173JB

Windhoek, 20 October 1996

Dear Bob,

We have received the wheelchairs! Here we do say: "Baie Dankie" for thank you!
Some of these have already been sent to the Homes. You can't imagine how happy the new users are !
We allocated the other, very useful goods among the two homes as well.
On behalf of children and staff of both Cheshire Homes I would like to thank you for your kind efforts to obtain and organise transport of these wheelchairs and spareparts.

I was extremely impressed by the efficient, prompt and friendly manner you have been dealing with this matter.
It would indeed be a good idea to make use of the services of Air Namibia more often. We will keep you posted.

For your information enclosed please find our annual report for1996 and some additional information.
I wish you all success with your good work!

With kind regards and best wishes,

Ingrid Gerhardt

One of the many 'Thank you' letters from overseas

Some of the buildings were little more than mud huts, but the children and adults residing there and the staff caring for them made them places touched with love and smiles. On one occasion, Bob and Nel found a group of people standing closely together and obviously waiting for their arrival. As they drew near the people began to sing. The sound was clear and beautiful; perfect harmonies rose up as the traditional welcoming song filled the air. The travellers felt tears well up in their eyes as they knew they would never forget this time. So many new friends were made. It was especially good to meet two of Penny's sons, her sister Ruth, a pharmacist, her other sister Ivy and Ivy's husband, James, who later became chairman of the nearby Westwood Cheshire home.

It was hard to leave a place which, although so different from England, had somehow seemed to fit them so easily. They left with promises to come back one day.

Bob continued with his work for a couple of years, but then began to wonder if, at 71, he might slow down a bit. Nel had retired from her job at the Marlborough School in 1990. And he couldn't keep on loading lorries, rushing up the motorway to Heathrow and so on for ever. Perhaps this was the time to hand over the administration to someone younger. He told the committee of his decision and after a time a new man, Philip Allan, took over the job in 1997. Bob worked alongside him for a while and then began to spend much more time at home in Stonesfield – where he knew he'd find plenty to do.

Towards the end of 1998, the postman dropped a long cream envelope through the letterbox. Unknown to Bob, wheels had been turning within the Leonard Cheshire Foundation because his superiors and colleagues had decided that his hard work ought to be recognised. Bob bent down, picked up the letter and turned it over. It was addressed to him and was stamped with a Royal Crest. Goodness – what could this be about? He showed it to Nel before sitting down at the kitchen table to see what was inside.

It was an invitation to Buckingham Palace to receive an MBE for his 'Services to Disabled People Overseas'. Bob stared at the page. He could hardly believe what he was reading. He'd worked hard, yes, but he'd enjoyed the work – he got enormous satisfaction from being able to help so many people in need of the equipment that he could supply. He knew how much they appreciated it, but the job really wasn't too difficult – and here he was, being honoured for it! The letter said that he was to tell no-one until afterwards. Nel wondered how they were ever going to contain themselves? Why, that very day they were going to a coffee morning at Avis Ushaw's house. They would have to chat with friends without a mention of this thrilling secret.

Somehow, they managed to behave normally for the next couple of months. It turned out that Bob and Nel were allowed two guests to accompany them to the palace and they chose their son Rob and his wife Maggie. It was a relief to be able to talk about the coming event with them. Nel and Maggie of course had to decide what they would wear on the great day. A happy Christmas came and went and soon it was February and time for them all to travel to London for this very special occasion.

After spending the night in a hotel and an evening visit to a cinema, they took a taxi to Buckingham Palace where the family felt enormously privileged to pass through the gates where previously they had stood and looked at the building with other tourists. They waited in the courtyard for a short while before being ushered into the reception area. Here, identities were confirmed and the guests mingled in respectful anticipation. Then Bob and Nel, Rob and Maggie found themselves in the midst of an excited group of people who were seeing the inside of the Queen's home for the first time.

As they were led up the staircase, they gazed at the huge paintings on the walls and the beautiful plasterwork above them. They walked along a landing until they reached the ballroom where the ceremony would take place. An orchestra played gentle music as the guests found their seats. Bob was one of over 100 people who were there to receive their awards. The recipients were ushered into an annexe at the side of the ballroom. Here, a man dressed in a colonel's uniform addressed them. He explained what would happen when they were called by the Lord Chamberlain. He told them where to stand and said they must stay quite still; the Queen would come to them. "Then," said the colonel, "she will offer you her hand and you will shake it."

After this, he told them that Her Majesty had been unwell that morning so the Duke of Edinburgh might take her place. It was uncertain. The guests waited and wondered. Bob found himself next to the England fast bowler, Angus Fraser, who was also there to receive an MBE. Having always been a cricket fan, this was a real bonus.

The orchestra stopped playing; everyone was asked to stand as they heard the first strains of the National Anthem. A small, elegant lady entered the room, flanked by two Ghurka orderly officers and everyone realised that they would indeed receive their award from the Queen after all. Five members of the Queen's Body Guard, the Yeomen of the Guard, were in position on the dais.

The investiture ceremony began. Bob knew that his time with his sovereign would be very short so he must make it a moment to remember. As the Queen moved towards him, her equerry spoke a few words of background information. Then Bob shook her by the hand and told her he

A moment to remember: the Queen greets Bob at his investiture, 1998
Reproduced by permission of British Ceremonial Arts

thought Leonard Cheshire had been a wonderful man. The Queen agreed with Bob and made him a Member of the Most Excellent Order of the British Empire. A photographer took pictures of each recipient as they received their awards. Her Majesty moved on to the next person and Bob sat down, looking at his star-shaped medal lying in its blue box.

All too soon, the afternoon was over. Reluctantly, the guests left the palace. Bob and his family decided that what was needed was a celebration meal and went in search of a restaurant. Walking through St James's Park they came face to face with a person with two little dogs on leads. They immediately recognised him as the actor, Martin Clunes. Nel, particularly, was thrilled to meet him and, still full of bonhomie after a wonderful afternoon, she took him by the shoulders and exclaimed, "You were wonderful last night!" Martin looked pleasantly startled and rather bemused, until the family explained that the film they had seen was 'Shakespeare in Love' in which he'd taken part. "Oh, that!" he chuckled. Then he was very gracious, thanked them sincerely for their compliments and went on his way. For Bob and Nel, it had been a nice little finale to an unforgettable afternoon.

CHAPTER 17

Back in the village, the Hains could at last tell their friends and neighbours about the MBE. And of course, news spreads like a forest fire in a small community. Bob was taken by surprise sometimes as he was congratulated by so many people he met. Having the award and the photograph on top of the bookcase was a constant reminder of his work and the people he'd got to know. Bob and Nel kept in touch with many of them, including Penny in Zimbabwe. They knew she would welcome them back at any time and they began to think that perhaps it was time now for a second visit.

During 1998 they made their plans and the following year saw them flying off once more to Harare. This time it would be more of a holiday, and as well as revisiting some of the homes and projects they knew, they would stay at Penny's home, see more of the country and go 'On Safari'.

Penny met them at the airport and quickly settled Bob and Nel into her home. Sitting on the veranda of her house and watching the birds and butterflies as they fluttered around the Jacaranda trees or sharing a delicious meal made them feel comfortable and very welcome. Penny grew her own oranges and lemons, sugar cane, bananas, pumpkins, cabbage, guavas, pawpaw and mangoes and her housekeeper, Gloria, helped her in using them to produce plenty of delicious dishes.

Their host accompanied her guests on a flight to the beautiful Kariba Lake where a long cruise across the water enabled sightings of buffalo and impala on an island and a profusion of birds. This was followed by a visit to Kariba Heights, where Bob and Nel gazed in awe at the massive wall of the dam as it shimmered in the heat of the morning. Much cooler was a sunset cruise that evening where, under the glow of a red, orange and deep purple sky, elephants, hippos, zebra, impala and water buck quietly drank or waded in the shallows of the lake. Nel wrote in her diary that they were having 'such a heavenly time'. In their hotel, they were entertained by African dancers; on Sunday, attending a nearby church, they were amazed by the sheer beauty of the singing; on their final morning they went to a crocodile farm where the oldest animal was 91 years and they were told that croc-tails were a great delicacy on menus. It had indeed been a wonderful time.

Back in Harare, it was time to see again some familiar projects and people. Bob and Nel were given a huge welcome at the Chiota Project for disabled children. Previously, there had been nothing in the way of shelter except for trees; now, they were delighted to see a brick-built assembly room.

Staff and workers at the Chiota Project, Zimbabwe, in 1998

Some children were taught to sew school uniforms which were sold to a local school; others were involved in gardening or garden tool-making, chicken farming and chain-link fencing. There was much singing and hand-shaking and before the couple left a blind girl proudly showed her hand-knitted baby clothes. Bob and Nel promised to send her more wool with Penny, along with fabric for the dressmakers, before they bid reluctant farewells.

It was so good to meet friends at the Westwood Cheshire Home – again, a Home for children. Here as well, a new building had appeared and the second stage foundations were in place. They hadn't expected so much wonderful progress. A week or so later, Bob and Nel heard that the Home's fridge had broken down. Ah, this was something they could help with! Bob arranged for Sister Illumina, the Head of Home, to drive him and Nel to a store where they chose and paid for a new fridge, to be delivered that day or the next. When they arrived at the Home, Sister Illumina told the children about this and it was very touching to hear so many little voices saying, "Thank you for the fridge … thank you for the fridge … thank you for the fridge …" It had been so easy for Bob to do but meant so much to the little residents.

More buildings had been erected at the Shelter Trust which cared for girls disowned by their parents for becoming pregnant. The Trust was teaching them skills to help them survive as a single parent, much of their work being done on sewing and knitting machines. Later, when their babies had grown and were at school, the mothers could go back to work at the Trust, producing items for sale.

The second week of the holiday saw the Hains travelling to Chivero Lake, where they stayed in the aptly-named Hippo Lodge before heading off for Great Zimbabwe. Here, they had a real adventure when, halfway into the jungle, their vehicle suffered a puncture. Bob tried his best but just couldn't persuade the spare tyre to drop from the under-carriage so they drove for two miles on the flat tyre to a junction. Here, a Park Attendant managed to remove the tyre but it too was flat. Dusk was falling fast and Bob, Nel and Penny were becoming anxious. The attendant radioed for help and after an hour, a jeep arrived. The luggage and passengers were settled aboard the new vehicle and there followed a journey of almost 30 miles.

The ground underneath them was very rough; far above them a half moon shone in a star-sprinkled sky; all around the sounds of the jungle and the bush filled the air. Darting dots of light pinpricked the darkness as hundreds of fireflies went about the night's business. The driver put his foot down hard on the accelerator and it became quite a feat to remain on the back seat of the jeep as the wheels sped over the potholes and ruts of the track. Bumping into each other, Bob and Nel held on tightly to the suitcases and provisions. Nel saw a pack of wild dogs out hunting; three zebra and a hyena flashed past and a python slithered across the path in front of the jeep. This was so exciting – she imagined her grandchildren's faces when she would tell this tale! After picking up a few others so that eventually nine people sat in or hung on to the jeep, the party arrived, exhausted but exhilarated, at Mana Pools from where they would go on a game drive the next day.

The holiday was almost over. Bob and Nel had seen all kinds of animals; had eaten meals cooked outside on an open fire; had been into caves and up mountains. They had, for a while, been part of a very different culture which had accepted and welcomed them. But a few days later they said their farewells, boarded the plane for Gatwick and flew home to a garden filled with the daffodils and primroses of an English spring.

CHAPTER 18

The Millennium began to peep over the edge of the 1990s and village folk wondered how they should mark it. They would never see another so they must do something very special. The Parish Council put on its thinking cap.

Stonesfield had so much to celebrate with its rich history, interesting characters and diverse activities. Why, you could almost fill a book about it! Yes…of course, why not write one? This was an excellent idea. Everyone could be asked to recall their memories of times past and more recent happenings, thus ensuring that as well as creating a fascinating book, these accounts would be set down in print and not lost to future generations. It wouldn't be the first book to be written about the village, but it would be the first to be written by the community.

Richard Chancellor, who had already published some material about Stonesfield, and six other people with appropriate skills would have the main task of writing and editing the book. Bob Hain felt very fortunate to be one of this group. But nothing could happen without contributions from as many villagers as possible.

Work on the new project began in earnest. Before long people were flicking through photo albums, looking out old newspaper articles ("I know I had it somewhere…") and rummaging in drawers for souvenirs. From the joy of being given a bag of sweets and an orange by American soldiers visiting the school in 1944, to the terror of the tall, grey-coated ghostly figure who was supposed to appear on the road to Fawler, there were tales to tell and almost-forgotten memories to revive. Bob found a good photograph of the village walk to Swinbrook and Nel provided as much information as she could about the Choral Society.

Every group, from the Stonesfield Society (a society devoted to learning more about the arts and environment) through the Badminton and Volleyball Clubs to the Wine Club and the Sea Angling Club – how many other land-locked villages could boast one of these? – was asked to write about their history and activities. A great number of villagers provided vital information; some of these were interviewed and their stories recorded on tape and, later, onto CDs. Even more lent documents and photographs. After much writing, rewriting and editing the book was almost complete. The final entry consisted of the thoughts of eight children from the primary school who had been asked to write down their ideas about how life in Stonesfield might be in 50 or even 100 years' time.

So what kind of title would encapsulate the information within such a book? Despite its agricultural history and glove-making trade, the village was most famous for its roofing slates of Jurassic limestone, mined here for over 300 years. It would be good to weave a title around this local yet internationally known industry. The words gradually presented themselves: the title would be 'Stonesfield from slates to chips.'

The 'chips' were microchips. In 1969, at the beginning of the electronics revolution, a man named Colin Sanders had seen the possibilities in computers and

The millennium book

created a firm, eventually called Solid State Logic. It was a very successful enterprise, winning the Queen's Award for Export Achievement. Colin erected an individually designed building to house his firm in Churchfields and became a very popular man who was good to the village. In 1999 news of his sudden death in a helicopter crash left a saddened community quite bereft. By then, Solid State Logic had moved out of Stonesfield but the Churchfields building was still full of life, having been taken over by Torex, another successful electronics firm.

So the authors felt that this title illustrated perfectly the link between past and present, showing that while Stonesfield valued its history it could still be right up to date. The book was finally published. It had been difficult to decide which photographs to choose and when to stop tweaking the text, but the finished result was a fine book and the residents couldn't wait to own a copy.

During the first decade of the new century, Bob and Nel went to Canada to see a Malaysian student who had previously stayed with them in Stonesfield. Now Arunika was married with a little daughter, and the Hains were made very welcome and enjoyed seeing some of the beauty of her adopted country. Back home, they continued to enjoy village life and all it meant to them. Bob was always willing to help with any jobs that needed doing, so when he heard of Peter Clifton's idea for a village transport scheme he pricked up his ears. Peter knew that some other communities had

Visiting Arunika and daughter Anisha in Halifax, Nova Scotia

schemes where volunteer drivers took people without transport to medical appointments. Country bus timetables didn't always match appointment times and some elderly people weren't able to walk to a Stop and climb onto a bus. So if there was no family member or neighbour to give a lift, a taxi was the only option until now.

Bob joined the scheme along with other volunteers and it became a success. But it wasn't too long before he had a few health problems and began to feel less robust. His doctor told him it would be better if he were to give up his car and reluctantly, Bob agreed. Gradually, he and Nel realised that Four Acres, with its big, beautiful garden was becoming too much for them to care for. They had always loved the house but didn't want the pleasure it gave them to become, instead, a burden.

A bungalow in Busby Close, not far away as the crow flies, came up for sale. Bob and Nel thought it was perfect. It was light, warm and airy inside, and outside, a smaller garden. They could have some good raised flowerbeds here. Close neighbours were familiar faces; things couldn't be better.

The move was made. Leaving Four Acres was a wrench but the decision was right. The Hains settled in quickly, deciding to have help in the house and garden so that they could continue to enjoy life. They still take an active part in village life, belonging to a good number of its organisations, and of course are regular worshippers at St James the Great. Wednesdays see them at the Stonesfield Lunch Club where they can meet with friends, enjoy some entertainment and a good meal provided by the kind volunteers.

In 2013 Bob and Nel celebrated their 65th wedding anniversary with a party. And in true Hain fashion they only sent out one invitation. That was to everyone in the village – anyone who wanted to come could just turn up, knowing they'd be given a warm welcome. Plenty of people did turn up to enjoy food, drink and good company, and to help this well-loved couple make it another day to remember.

When people like Bob and Nel have given so much to a place it is not forgotten. Now that they need help in various ways people don't hesitate to offer it. Bob has found life in Stonesfield very good and says, "I can't imagine where else I'd have found such a supportive community." But probably, the truth is likely to be that 'the smile you give out comes back to you'.

Sixty-five years together! Bob and Nel, August 2013